SILK
PAINTING

◆

*Dedicated to my mother Mona Wauchope
who started me silk painting, and without whom I would
never have finished this book*

Above: Mop-ups made into lampshade and cushion (see 'Chapter 9' and page 95)
Previous page: Painting with water using an eye-dropper combined with serti method

SILK PAINTING

STEP–BY–STEP

A GUIDE TO TECHNIQUES AND MATERIALS

LIZ WAUCHOPE

PHOTOGRAPHS BY MARAH WESTON

CASSELL

Thanks to:
Geraldine Clarke, Linda Clair
and especially to Kirsten Lindsay
for all our mutual discoveries in
silk painting and selling, Pauline
Clack for our joint efforts on the
fabric pictured on page 16: my
husband, Greg Ramsey, for his
support over the years, and his
argumentative proofreading of
this book.

Above: Detailed serti method silk, with silk painting equipment
Cover: Lasseter's Reef, gutta and paint decoration over mop-up

A CASSELL BOOK

First published in the UK
1993 by Cassell
Villiers House
41/47 Strand
London
WC2N 5JE

Distributed in the United States by
Sterling Publishing Co., Inc.
387 Park Avenue South,
New York, NY 10016-8810

First published in Australasia in 1992 by
Simon & Schuster Australia
20 Barcoo Street, East Roseville NSW 2069

A Paramount Communications Company
Sydney, New York, London, Toronto, Tokyo, Singapore

© Liz Wauchope

British Library
Cataloguing-in-Publication Data

A catalogue record for this book is available from the British Library

ISBN 0-304-34268-8

Designed by Fox Badger Ferret
Typeset in Australia by Fox Badger Ferret
Printed in Hong Kong by South China Printing Company
Project co-ordinated by Elizabeth Halley

✦ CONTENTS ✦

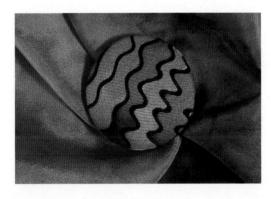

Brooch (see page 98) and rock-salted scarf (see page 51)

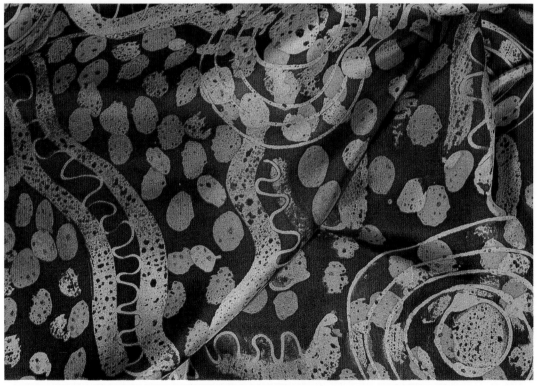

Above: Batik (see 'Variations', page 64)
Below: Batik (see 'Chapter 8')

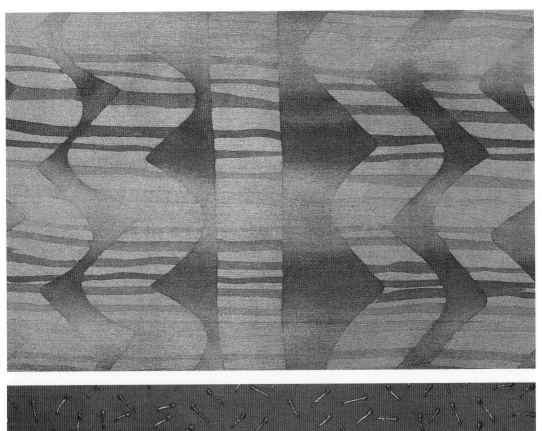

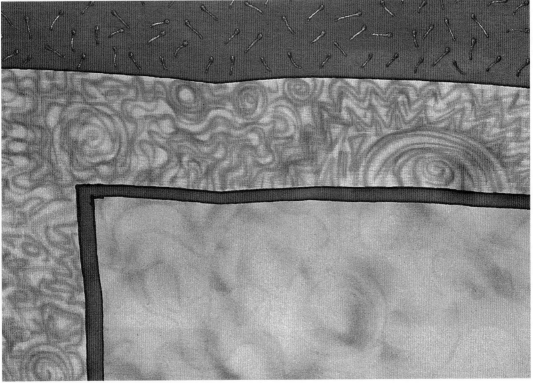

Above: Antifusant (see 'Variations', page 57)
Below: Fabric pen and diffusant (see page 58)

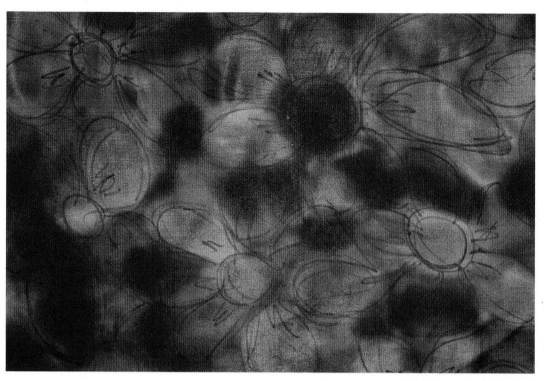

Eye-dropper and fabric pen (see pages 54, 92)

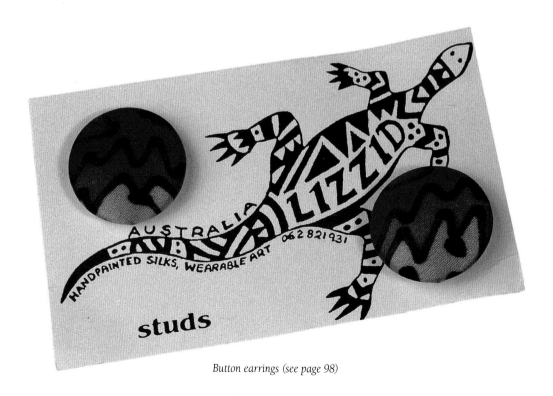

Button earrings (see page 98)

Mop-ups – well blended (see 'Variations', page 68)

Above: 'Kangaroos' (see page 87)
Below: 'Gum Blossom', on antifusant (see page 56)

'Lorikeets' (see page 87)

'Cockatoos' (see page 90)

'Gum Blossom', serti method (see pages 56, 88)

Above: Wet against dry technique (see 'Variations', page 53)
Left: Sugar syrup, splattering technique (see page 72)   Right: Rock-salt scarf (see page 51)

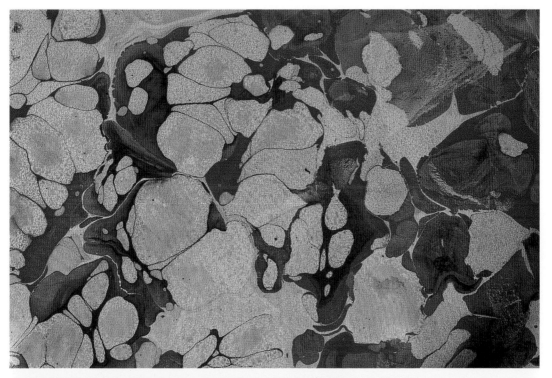

Above: Simple marbling – uncombed (see page 77)
Below: Things to make (see 'Chapter14')

Above: Desert Opal Mulga, printed by Pauline Clack over mop-up by Liz Wauchope (see 'Chapter 12', page 81)
Below: Desert Opal Caterpillars, printed by Pauline Clack over mop-up by Liz Wauchope (see 'Chapter 12', page 81)

INTRODUCTION

Painting on silk, using paints designed specifically for silk and wool, is quite different from any other type of fabric painting. Silk paints and dyes are translucent rather than opaque like the thicker types of fabric paints, and they sink into the fibres rather than sit on the surface. This means that the unique sheen of the silk is preserved, not blotted out, and the fabric remains soft and flexible. These paints don't just sit on the fabric or have to be coerced into movement. I find the process peaceful and satisfying, almost meditative, in the flow of paints across the fabric.

The colours of silk paints are strong and vibrant (but can be made soft and pastel with dilution), and are colour-fast so that they are both washable and dry-cleanable.

The combination of the silk itself and the brilliant colours of the silk paints allows even the most un-skilled novice to create stunningly beautiful fabrics.

Silk painting by the serti method requires that the silk be stretched tautly on a frame so that a resist, called 'gutta', can be drawn on to it to outline a design. This stops the paint from bleeding beyond the designs, so that separately coloured areas can be formed. It is a lot like drawing an outline and colouring in, and just as easy once you master the gutta pen!

Painting on silk of course originated in China, along with silk itself. When silk weaving was introduced to France in the sixteenth century, silk painting came with it. Like marbling, it was largely forgotten for a time, and then revived in this century. Most of the techniques in this book have been derived from techniques discovered, or rediscovered, in France.

Silk painting of this kind has been in Australia since the late 1970s. In the last ten years it has gone from a rarely seen craft to an epidemic of nationwide proportions. One of the reasons for this is that it is so easy to obtain a satisfying result.

I discovered the craft by accident. I had had nothing to do with any kind of artistic endeavour, except for an envious appreciation of other people's talents, since school. In 1982 I took my mother to Hahndorf, an historic village and tourist centre in South Australia, where we saw Annie Ubeda painting in the traditional serti style. Mum, who has been interested in all sorts of crafts for a long time, bought the equipment and we both experimented. I was hooked, and over the next ten years my life was taken over by a hobby which turned into a serious, intensely rewarding, all-consuming full-time occupation.

How to Use This Book

'Part One' provides detailed information on the basics of silk painting. The technical side of this craft is very important if you are going to achieve a good result. It would be disappointing to see your work fade away because you did not fix the colour properly into the silk. While this part is directed to beginners, it also contains many points of interest for experienced painters, including aspects which may not have been encountered before.

'Part Two' contains chapters on specific techniques. Each chapter begins with a step-by-step guide to a basic project to illustrate that technique, and then briefly mentions a host of variations which you can try.

I suggest that you proceed through the book in this way:

1. Read 'Chapter 1' and buy any materials that you will need.

2. Follow 'Chapter 2', 'Chapter 3', 'Chapter 4' and 'Chapter 5' in succession, step by step, to paint a piece of silk and test out your knowledge of the basics.

3. Try the first step-by-step guide in each of the chapters in 'Part Two' before going on to the variations in that chapter.

Happy Painting!

◆

1
MATERIALS

The basic materials that you will need for silk painting are outlined in this chapter.

SILK

There are many different types and qualities of silk and all can be painted. If you are using the French silk paints, you must use 100 per cent silk, or a combination of silk and wool, or else the colour will eventually wash out. Natural silk is best to start with, because coloured silks will change the colour of the paint. Some silks also come with a starchy sizing in them and feel stiff. You will need to wash the silk and dry it before painting on it if this is the case, otherwise the sizing can prevent the paint from entering the silk properly. If you are not sure if there is sizing, wash it anyway.

Silk comes in different weights, commonly measured in grams per metre by the Japanese 'momme' which is about 4.3 grams per metre (a little over a tenth of an ounce per yard). Thus, a '4 momme' is lighter and therefore finer than an '8 momme'. There is a wide variety of weaves, and each has a different surface texture. You will find that the paint and gutta can react differently with each weight and weave of silk.

Habutai (or Jap), and Pongee

These are examples of plain weaves, the simplest of the three forms of weaving. (The other weaving forms are twills and satins.) I find that the lightweight habutai, known as 'paj', is a little too fine and easy to damage, but many painters like it because it has a greater sheen. Pongee is a similar type but made from spun silk. The lighter weights of all three are a little too flimsy for clothes, although they can be used as linings. The heavier weights of habutai can be made into light blouses and shirts.

I think that the best silk for basic scarves is an 8, 10 or 12 momme habutai. Although a 4 momme will do, it is very fine and threads will catch and pull easily. On habutai the paint runs, or bleeds, a long way, and gutta sinks into the fabric more easily than into heavier silks. Since habutai is a light weave, it does not absorb as much paint, and so the colours end up paler than the same dilutions would on a heavier type of silk.

Chiffon and Georgette

These are two more examples of plain weave, but are woven in a looser way so that they are filmy or sheer, and shrink more when washed. Georgette has a rougher, more crepe-like surface than chiffon. Since you can see right through them they are best used for scarves or overclothes. Gutta penetrates easily, although you need to watch that the irregularities in the weave do not result in gaps in your lines. Paint does not seem to bleed as far as with the smoother habutai, and the colours tend to look paler than on other weaves because the fabric is so flimsy.

Crepe de chine

Another plain weave, crepe has a lovely sheen and is quite easy to paint and to sew. Heavier than the ones discussed so far, it is excellent for both scarves and for clothing. Gutta and paint may need to be slightly more dilute to ensure that the gutta penetrates the fibre and to avoid wasting paint. This fabric is able to hold more paint than lighter weaves and so you can achieve very intense hues.

Twill

Twill weaves all have a diagonal line pattern across the fabric. There are many different silks woven on this basis, but a lightweight twill suitable for scarves and blouses or shirts is sold simply as 'twill'. It is very shiny, soft and slippery and therefore hard to sew, but it is a delight to paint. It holds the paint well so that the colours are more intense than on a habutai, and gutta on twill easily forms an effective wall into the fabric.

Satin and Satin Crepe

Satin is the third major category of weave, and its main characteristic is a smooth surface which is so shiny that it ripples with light. Like the twill, a simple satin is so slippery that it is hard to sew — but easy to paint. It is good for scarves and lightweight clothing. It is my favourite silk for ties and bow ties.

There is also a satin crepe which is satin on one side and crepe on the other. This is heavier than the plain satin, and thus richer and easier to sew. It requires slightly more care in using the gutta, which you could dilute a little more than usual to ensure penetration. You do not need to use as strong a mixture of paint on satin crepe as on satin, to achieve the same intensity of colour. Satin crepe is not suitable for scarves only because the two sides of the fabric look so different from each other, but it is fine for all other projects.

Noil and Raw Silk

Raw silk and noil are very heavy weights with no sheen. Noil has little flecks of brown matter through it. Neither fabric is suitable for scarves, but both are good for jackets and pants, and other outer garments. They will soak up a lot of paint, which will not bleed much at all. As with all the very thick silks, you will need to dilute the paint with a lot more water, even adding up to 90 per cent water. This is because the thick weave soaks up so much paint that the colours become intense more easily, and some of the paint will inevitably wash out if there is too much of it for the fibres to hold, so it wastes paint to have the colours in normal strengths.

In addition, gutta does not penetrate the tight thick weave as easily, and so your usual dilution will be less effective in keeping the paint from bleeding through the lines. Thus on this silk you will have to dilute it more, and make very thick gutta lines, even gutta both sides of the silk — or use hot wax instead of gutta.

Jacquard

Similar in appearance to a damask tablecloth, a jacquard is a fabric with a repeating picture or pattern woven into it. The pattern is sometimes raised above the surface, or more commonly it is shinier than the background. There is a huge variety, from simple lines and geometric shapes to complex flowers and paisley. There are lightweight satiny jacquards and very heavy raw silk jacquards. Because there is such a variety it is hard to generalise about their reaction to the paints and gutta. Basically, the heavier and more complex the jacquard the more dilute you will need the gutta and the paint. Special care needs to be taken when using gutta on a jacquard, because the weave is tighter where the pattern is, and so it is harder for the gutta to penetrate evenly.

Availability

There are many and varied prices for silk, and the variation is not only between types but also between suppliers. You can get silk from most retail fabric stores, and you will probably only want to buy small quantities at a time at first. However, if you get into silk painting in a big way, buying silk wholesale will further reduce the price. You will then have to buy in bulk, usually at least 20 m (22 yd) at a time.

SILK PAINTS

True 'silk paints' are designed specifically for use on silk and wool. They do not work at all on synthetic material, and will wash out completely, no matter what you do, if the material is not natural fibre. There is little point in using this particular type of paint on cotton, although it can permanently colour the cotton, because the translucence and fast-spreading qualities of the paints would be lost.

There are several brands of silk paint available, and more being added to the market all the time. The main differences lie in the colour ranges (see 'Brand Names'). There is no white: to get white areas on the silk you do not paint those spaces. Most of the techniques in this book will work in a similar way with all brands of silk paints.

There are also powder dyes which are not specific to silk but which can be used in the same way and have many of the properties of silk paints.

See the section on 'Brand Names' at the back of the book for a brief evaluation of some of the types of silk paints and powder dyes available.

You may also want to use alcohol for diluting the paint. Mixed 50:50 with water, this makes some of the techniques such as rock-salting much more effective. Unfortunately, it is not possible to get pure alcohol in some countries without a doctor's prescription. I use ethyl rubbing alcohol, or methylated spirits instead of pure alcohol, but they are very smelly!

Silk paints and powder dyes are not toxic, but do stain, so you should protect your hands from paint with disposable plastic gloves (available in handy packs from supermarkets). It is difficult to paint delicate work wearing rubber gloves, so the thin plastic ones are best.

GUTTA

This is the resist which acts as an outliner to draw your design on the silk. It prevents the paint from spreading from one area of the silk to another. It can also be used purely as decoration or for emphasis. Its basis is latex or vegetable gum, depending on the type. Its function is similar to that of wax in a batik in that it sinks into the fabric and acts as a wall or barrier through which the paint will not travel (unless you have drawn your line too thinly, or with gaps in it!).

Gutta stays at a usable consistency without heat: this is a distinct advantage over wax in a batik. It is also easier to learn to draw fine lines with gutta in an applicator pen than it is with hot wax in the wax applicator (called a 'tjanting' or 'canting') for batik.

Spirit-Based Gutta

The most commonly available guttas are spirit-based, diluted with white spirit, Shellite or dry-cleaning fluid.

Clear spirit-based gutta can be removed from the silk, once you have finished your painting, by washing the silk in white spirit or Shellite.

There are pre-mixed coloured guttas available as well as clear gutta, and these are

he same way, but generally need
dded. The most common colours
gold and silver. You can also make
your own coloured gutta by adding, drop by
drop, glass enamel paint to clear gutta, but this
is not as good because it gets very dribbly.

Coloured guttas look good, but are harder
to use because they tend to dribble more (it is
harder to control their flow), and you have to
be able to draw very thin lines because you
cannot take the gutta out without losing the
colour as well. This also means that these types
of coloured guttas cannot be dry-cleaned.
There are dry-cleanable spirit-based coloured
guttas available in France – see 'List of
Suppliers'.

Some brands of metallic spirit-based guttas
are neither washable nor dry-cleanable, and
should only be used on wallhangings, lampshades and other items which are not to be
washed – see the section on 'Brand Names'.

Water-Based Gutta

By contrast, water-based metallic guttas are
both dry-cleanable and washable, and result
in a line that is clear and full of richness and
colour.

The gum content in water-based gutta can
be removed or softened by washing: the colour
from the gutta remains behind. Adding
washing soda to the water helps in this process
of removing the stiffness of the gum, but you
need to be careful not to soak the fabric for too
long in the soda solution as the colours you
have painted on the silk may run, as a result of
the action of the soda.

These guttas can be quite difficult to use,
and you will need to refer to 'Chapter 3' before
you try them. They take much longer to dry
than spirit-based guttas (half an hour or so in
the sun, as opposed to less than a minute), and
some may even need to be ironed to set them
before you attempt to paint within the lines.
However, I think that the beauty of the lines

produced and the fact that the finished silk is
both washable and dry-cleanable far outweigh
the difficulties.

APPLICATOR PENS AND NIBS

These are used to apply the gutta. The pen is a
plastic tube with a screw-on nozzle, to which
you attach a metal nib with masking tape.
Nibs come in many sizes for a thicker or
thinner line.

While the nibs always come with a
correctly sized wire to seal the hole, I almost
inevitably lose these, so I keep a supply of
either fuse wire or beading wire, and pins for
thicker (size 8) nibs.

Always ensure the hole is plugged by wire
or a pin when you put your pen away at the
end of the day, or the nib will clog.

Apparently you can make your own
applicator by rolling a piece of paper into a
cone with a small hole at the pointy end. I
have never done this, however, as I find the
pens to be excellent.

FIXING AGENTS

Most of the silk paints and dyes are extremely
susceptible to water until the colour has been
set, or fixed, in the fabric. Even if your
painting has been lying around 'air curing' for
days and days, if a spot of water touches it, a
permanent mark will be made. Until the paint
or dye has been fixed, the fabric is not
washable. There are several ways to ensure
colour fastness, and each brand will specify the
processes available to it, the times required for
steaming, and the dilutions and times required
for chemical fixing.

Chemical Fixatives

Those brands of silk paints which can be set
by a chemical instead of by steaming, all have
their own particular type of fixative to set the
colour. Most of these seem to be a mixture of
acetic acid, or vinegar, and water, but because

the acid or alkaline balance in the different brands of paints may vary, it is safer to use the fixative which goes with that brand. You should follow the instructions for dilution and use which are on the bottle.

Those brands which have a chemical fixative say that you do not need to steam and need only use the fixative, but the trouble with this is that some of the colour washes out of the silk while you are soaking it in the fixative bath, so you can never get the really vibrant colours from using fixative alone. Therefore, I always steam my silk or stabilise the colour in the microwave first, and then soak it in a fixative bath.

Steaming

Steaming actually enhances the vibrancy of the colours and, in addition, is more effective in setting them. So there is less chance of the colour running both while you are fixing and whenever you wash it afterwards.

You can use an ordinary saucepan or a pressure cooker to steam the silk (the advantage of a pressure cooker is that you can steam for half the time), but you can only do one scarf at a time and cannot do big lengths of silk. This method permanently presses the folds into the silk. It is also fairly easy for water to get in and ruin your work this way. Even so, in the beginning you will find it is sufficient, and far less expensive than buying a commercial steamer.

The best thing if you are going to do lots of silk painting is to get a proper steamer: you can order them through the outlets listed in the 'List of Suppliers', or you can get one made up by a sheet metal worker, using the illustrations in 'Chapter 5'. They are very expensive, whichever way you do it, because stainless steel is used. However, you can save some money by having one made up, and this also means you can get a bigger one done so that it can accommodate wider silk.

Microwaving plus fixative

This is a simple but effective way of ensuring much better colour retention than using fixative alone. It is less liable to crease the fabric or to produce watermarks than using a saucepan or pressure cooker. Basically the microwave is used as a steamer, and yet it is not enough on its own to set the colour completely: you will need to use a fixative bath to complete the process. Because microwaving can scorch the silk, or even set it on fire, it is important to follow the instructions given in 'Chapter 5'.

Ironing

Unlike the thicker fabric paints used for painting on other materials, silk paints cannot be fixed by ironing. There is a type of dye fixable by ironing which is very close to silk paints in the properties discussed above, except that it does not bleed as well – see 'Brand Names'.

WHITE SPIRIT OR SHELLITE

Both of these spirits are interchangeable for the purposes of silk painting. They are used to dilute spirit-based gutta, and to remove it from the silk completely if so desired.

You should wear rubber gloves if your hands are going to be in the spirit, for example when you are removing gutta, because it dries out the skin. Ordinary household washing-up gloves are fine, but they will swell and eventually disintegrate. Industrial-strength gloves from an occupational health and safety shop are better protection, and last longer.

It is best to work outside with white spirit or Shellite, so that you can avoid breathing the fumes as much as possible. Store the spirit in a shed outside if possible, especially if you have large quantities: it is highly flammable and quite dangerous.

Never use large quantities of Shellite or white spirit anywhere near an open flame: the fumes can ignite and cause the lot to explode. This happened to a friend of mine who was rinsing silk in a bath of Shellite in the kitchen sink and cooking lunch on a gas stove at the same time. The explosion knocked out the kitchen window, and she had severe burns on her hands and arms, which had been in the Shellite when it caught fire.

DIFFUSANT AND ANTIFUSANT

Diffusant, when added to the paint, makes it bleed faster and run more smoothly on the silk, thus making backgrounds easier to paint, and enhancing the rock-salt effect. Each silk paint brand has a pre-mixed diffusant in its range; or lyogen can be bought separately from craft suppliers, and substituted. Lyogen usually needs to be diluted with water, at least 50:50.

Antifusant is most commonly 10 per cent gutta mixed with white spirit or Shellite. When this is painted all over your silk and allowed to dry, any paint you then put on top of it will not bleed so far: it becomes like painting on paper.

FRAMES

Frames are used to stretch the silk so that it is taut enough to draw on easily and so that it does not touch the table, which would allow the paint to run under the gutta. You can buy frames made specifically for silk painting. These are adjustable and can be very good if you only do one painting at a time, and do not have space to store a lot of different sized frames.

It is easy, and less expensive, to make your own by buying boards from a timber store. See 'Chapter 2' for instructions on how to make your own frame.

PAINTBRUSHES

To begin with, you need at least one small paintbrush (about size 2 or 3), one medium one (about size 12, but with a good pointy tip)

and one very large one for backgrounds. As you become more involved in silk painting you may decide you want more of different sizes. Chinese bamboo-handled brushes with soft animal-hair bristles are best: they hold a lot of paint but always come to a sharp point as well. Although these have a tendency for the bristles to fall out, they are very inexpensive, and are easily repaired as the bristles come out in a single clump. I would strongly recommend you buy these because they allow for fine edges as well as large spaces. A foambrush suitable for borders and backgrounds is also available.

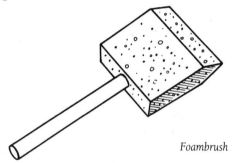

Foambrush

BUTCHER PAPER

This is used to wrap the silk in prior to steaming (unless you are using a microwave, in which case it is wrapped in absorbent kitchen paper). Butcher paper, or newsprint, is available from stationery stores by the sheet, which is satisfactory for a saucepan or pressure cooker, but when you get a proper steamer you really need a roll. This may be obtainable from your local newspaper printers, or from the contractor to whom they sell their end rolls (what is left from a huge roll of paper after a newspaper is printed).

RULER

A ruler is needed for drawing borders and straight lines. A piece of timber similar to that used in making your frame can be cut to a length a little wider than your largest frame: this makes ruling lines across the frame easier.

2

PREPARATION

This chapter is about designing your painting, and preparing your workspace, silk and frame. Careful preparation can save a great deal of trouble, and help avoid disasters once you start work. However, do not expect to paint perfectly on your first few tries. It took me two years before I painted anything I was willing to show to anyone other than my closest friends! If you are good at drawing, or other art forms, you will achieve better results much more quickly than that.

Materials
✦ drawing-pins or a lightweight staple gun and staples
✦ old newspapers
✦ pencils
✦ paper and an eraser if you wish to draw out a design first
✦ a ready-made frame; or 4 wooden boards cut to size, 8 nails, hammer, and, if desired, brackets and screws to strengthen the frame
✦ scissors
✦ shiny packaging tape, or masking tape
✦ jeweller's pliers or needle-nosed pliers and a flat knife, if you have used staples to attach your silk to the frame
✦ silk (a relatively lightweight jap, paj or habutai is best to start with)
✦ designs to trace, for example patterns used for stained glass

WORKSPACE
Even if you are working outside, or in the kitchen or laundry, it is helpful to make your workspace as clear and efficient as possible. If you can, use a flat table or workbench which is larger than the frame on which you will be painting your silk. It is safer to paint with the silk frame laid flat, so that paint does not dribble down over gutta lines. The extra space around your frame allows you to have your gutta pens, brushes and jars of paint and water within easy reach.

If you are working in a small area, on surfaces which can absorb the paint if you spill it, cover the tabletop or benchtop, and perhaps the floor, with old newspapers.

Working outside can be lovely, and means less worry about spillage. However, on hot sunny days your gutta may clog up more quickly, and the paints dry too rapidly on the silk for some effects, such as rock-salting. Fast drying paint also increases the danger of watermarks forming, so sit in the shade, or work inside.

DESIGNING YOUR PAINTING
Before you start, think about the design you wish to use. You might find it helpful to use a piece of paper to make a rough sketch, or even a true-to-size 'blueprint' which you can trace.

You may wish to trace or copy designs that are available for this purpose – stained glass pattern books are good to start with – and keep your eye open all the time for interesting things to use as a basis for designs. However, be careful about copyright!

Another idea is to take a photographic slide

or transparency and project it onto a glass door or window; then go outside, put paper against the glass and trace around the projected image.

If you are new to silk painting, it really is advisable to have very simple designs or pictures for your first efforts. Try something without too many small fiddly bits, which would be hard to draw in gutta, and hard to paint without going over the lines. Clear thick lines, and large shapes which are fully enclosed by a line, like the patterns used for stained glass, are ideal. Geometric shapes, scribble patterns like those we all did in primary school, and even large doodling patterns are all good to start with.

It pays to keep in mind that any open-ended shape, not enclosed by a full line, will allow the paint to bleed past the edge. This is fine if you want colours to run and blend randomly, but not if you want to keep them separate.

Remember to suit the size of your design to the size of the finished object you have in mind. If you are painting earrings, for example, you will need tiny patterns, whereas a large scarf will need a bigger design.

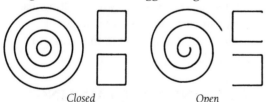

Closed   Open

Since obtaining a smooth background is one of the more difficult things to do, it is a good idea in the early stages to make an overall pattern so that you have a lot of separate areas to fill in, rather than one big space behind your main picture or pattern.

Designing with Borders

If you are painting a scarf, or a picture to be framed, it is a good idea to incorporate a border into the design. This lends a coherence

Background with separate areas

to your design so that it looks like a totally planned work, rather than just a piece of material. It helps to ensure that you do not draw integral parts of your design close to the staple holes and then have to cut them off. A border also guards against the problem of different colours running along the wood on the edge of your frame, and mixing where you do not want them to. It also means that you will not forget to take the lines of your design right to the edge, so that there are no gaps for the paint to run through.

When designing your painting, choose how wide you want your border to be: about 4 - 6 cm (1½ - 2½ in) wide is a good size in general terms, but it needs to suit the size of your piece. If you want to make sure your border meets at the corners, instead of crossing, you will need to follow steps 1 - 9 'Drawing a Border' in 'Chapter 3'. However, you can make crossing lines at the corners of your borders a feature of the design, and decorate inside them.

CHOOSING A COLOUR SCHEME

If you are using pencils and paper to sketch a design, use coloured pencils to try out colour schemes. This is a fairly long drawn out way of going about it, and you may prefer to do a test piece as outlined in 'Chapter 4'. This has the added advantage of showing you how the actual silk paint colours will mix and match.

The three books in the series *Designer's Guide to Colour* in the 'Supplementary Reading List' are excellent for showing colour combinations. Although the colour components shown in these books relate to printer's inks, you can use them as a guide to approximate proportions of silk colours needed to make the illustrated hues.

MAKING A FRAME

I use inexpensive pine planking bought cut to size from a timber merchant. Nail the frame together with the planks side on, as illustrated: this gives a narrower edge so that less silk is wasted and there is less likelihood of paint running along the wood to places where you do not want it to go. It also suspends the silk well above the table.

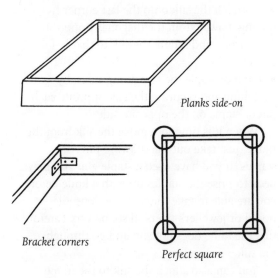

Planks side-on

Bracket corners

Perfect square

If you will be using your frame time and time again, you can strengthen it by screwing brackets into the corners as illustrated above.

If you want a perfectly square frame, join the corners in the way shown above.

If you are making a ver[...] for example 3 m (10 ft) b[...] you will need to nail a pi[...] across the bottom in the [...] below, so that the frame [...] inwards when you stretch the [...]

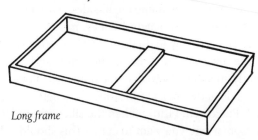

Long frame

Cover the uppermost edge of the frame with shiny packaging tape or masking tape to prevent the wood from staining. This will need to be cleaned, or replaced, after almost every painting, so that paint from one project does not transfer to the next. Therefore the shiny tape is better, because it can be wiped over with a wet cloth to remove paint.

WASHING THE SILK

Many silks are impregnated with a starchy sizing, or stiffening agent. This can make the paint sink into the fabric unevenly, so that you get blotchy marks and streaks. Not all silk will have sizing in it, but it is better to be sure than sorry and wash the silk before you attempt to paint on it.

This can be done by hand for a small piece of silk, but I find it easier to throw a large amount into the washing machine and run it through a normal cold-wash cycle as soon as I buy it, before I cut it up. In either case, a gentle soap powder or wool-wash mixture should be used rather than a harsh detergent.

Rinse the silk thoroughly and hang it out to dry, or attach it to the frame wet and let it dry there. It will stretch tightly as it dries if pinned on wet, which helps to provide a good flat surface to draw on. However, you can pin it on dry, with no real disadvantage. In either case it

necessary to iron the silk first because
stretching will pull the creases out enough
for the purpose of painting.

CUTTING THE SILK

Cut the silk to the size required so that it can
be attached to the frame on all sides, with an
overlap of approximately 1 cm ($^{1}/_{2}$ in).

✦ 1. The best way to do this is to hold a corner
of the silk against a corner of the frame, and
gently stretch the selvedge side of the silk along
one side of the frame to measure the length.

✦ 2. Put a 2 cm (1 in) nick in the silk with the
scissors where you want to cut it. This should
be at a point beyond the outside edge of the
frame, to accommodate the two 1 cm ($^{1}/_{2}$ in)
overlaps. Then tear the silk right across to the
other side.

✦ 3. Repeat this process to get the right width
of the silk piece.

✦ 4. Cut off any long loose threads from your
silk as these can drag across your painting and
smear it.

ATTACHING THE SILK
TO THE FRAME

The silk needs to be stretched fairly tightly and
evenly to ensure a stable surface on which to
paint, and to avoid scalloping of what should
be straight gutta lines.

Remember to stretch it as tightly as
possible if you are pinning or stapling dry silk,
but not quite so tightly if the silk is wet. This is
because it will shrink a little as it dries and the
pins may pop out or the staples tear the silk.

Try to keep the edge of the silk parallel to
the edge of the frame (that is, with roughly the
same amount of overlap all the way along), so
that your silk does not end up out of shape.

A staple gun is effective to pin the silk onto
the frame. This is available from hardware
sections in supermarkets, and is different from
the ordinary stapler used in the home or office
to join sheets of paper together. You do not
need a really heavy-duty one. Drawing-pins
can be used as a substitute.

If you are using a staple gun for the first
time, you will find it rather hard to apply
enough pressure. Don't worry: your hand will
soon strengthen. Be careful to place the gun
flush with the silk and frame, or staples may
fly off in all directions. Keep your fingers out
of the way!

✦ 1. Pin or staple one corner first. Stretch and
secure the silk about 10 cm (4 in) away on
either side of the first corner.

✦ 2. Stretch the silk away from that corner,
straight down one of the sides you just
secured, to the next corner. Secure the silk
with a pin or staple right on that corner.

✦ 3. Pin or staple the silk, in spaces about
10 cm (4 in) apart, all the way along the side
you just secured.

✦ 4. Repeat the process to stretch and pin or
staple an adjacent side, exactly as you did the
first side.

✦ 5. Stretch the silk onto the last corner by
pulling it away from the diagonally opposite
first corner, and secure the silk to that last
corner.

✦ 6. Pin or staple the remaining sides, by
stretching and securing the silk opposite each
pin or staple on the opposite side.

When it is time to remove the silk from the
frame, just take out the drawing-pins or
staples. If you have used a staple gun you may
need to prise the staples up with a knife before
you are able to take them out with needle-
nosed or jeweller's pliers. If so, be very careful
that the knife does not slip and go through
the silk.

You can also attach the silk to the frame
with masking tape, but this is not always
reliable, as it may lift off when the silk gets wet
during painting.

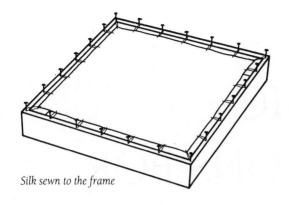

Silk sewn to the frame

Another way of attaching the silk is to sew it on. You can make this a simpler process by hammering nails or placing drawing-pins at intervals into the wooden frame, and using these as points to wind the thread around as you sew. This is a particularly good way of attaching scarves which have a ready-made handrolled hem: this ensures that the silk edge will not be damaged by large holes from staples or drawing-pins.

◆

3

BASIC INSTRUCTIONS FOR APPLYING GUTTA

This chapter covers the basic information you will need to use both spirit-based and water-based guttas. These substances can be tricky to master at first, but more than anything else they are what makes silk painting different from other forms of fabric painting, so it is well worth the effort. Gutta gives you control over the way in which the paint moves on the fabric better than any other method of outlining, with perhaps the exception of wax in a tjanting applicator. The advantage of gutta is that it is far easier to apply than wax.

If you have not done any silk painting before, I recommend that you start with clear spirit-based gutta because this is the easiest to use, and can also be removed after you have finished your painting. This can be a big help if you have made blobby lines (which all of us do at the beginning!). At least they will not remain sticky, even if you do still have thick white lines at the end of your project.

Materials
+ applicator pen
+ books to prop your design up to the level of the silk, or tape to attach the design to the back of the silk, if you are tracing
+ bottlebrush, of the size used to clean the teat on a baby's bottle
+ bottle of gutta
+ cotton buds (2 or 3)
+ eye-dropper
+ gutta pen nib – size 6 for thin lines, on habutai and other smooth silk; size 7 for medium lines, on lightweight to medium-weight silk; size 8 for thick lines on any silk (always use size 8 for very thick silk)
+ medium-size paintbrush
+ metal nailfile, if the gutta pen nib is rough
+ pipe-cleaners (2 or 3)
+ ruler, if you want a straight border
+ wooden skewer or other stirring implement which will fit in the pen

◆ Shellite or white spirit, up to 150 mL
(¹/₃ pt), if you are using spirit-based gutta
◆ small funnel to fit into the open neck of the
gutta pen
◆ small jar with a lid
◆ small strip of masking tape
◆ small wire sieve or tea-strainer, if you are
using water-based gutta
◆ Stanley knife or razor blade, if you are using
a new applicator pen
◆ water, up to 150 mL (¹/₃ pt), if you are using
water-based gutta
◆ fine wire, 5 cm (2 in), or a pin to insert in
the nib
◆ materials prepared from 'Chapter 2' (silk on
a frame, designs)
◆ small frame with silk stretched on it, to use
for testing

SPIRIT-BASED GUTTA

When you first buy it, spirit-based gutta
always needs diluting, and for clear gutta you
may need to add up to half as much again of
white spirit or Shellite (so you have 2 parts
gutta to 1 added part spirit).

If the gutta has been sitting on your shelf
for even just a few days, it may need up to this
much diluting again before you use it,
especially if you have left it in the applicator
pen instead of pouring it back into the bottle. I
always add a little more spirit to the gutta each
time I refill an applicator pen.

Black, silver and gold gutta will also need
thinning occasionally, but not as much, because
dilution will make the colour thinner as well.

You can always re-use the gutta you have
diluted, days or weeks later, provided that you
store it in a sealed bottle. Over a long period of
time it can become very thick and gluggy, and
in that case you will need to add more spirit,
shake the bottle vigorously, let it sit for an
hour or two, stir it up with a wooden skewer,
add more spirit, shake it ... and so on until you
have achieved a workable consistency.

*The most common problem with outlinin,
gutta which has not been diluted enough.*

This will cause it to sit on the surface oₗ ₗₕₑ
fabric rather than sink into the fibres and form
a wall to prevent the paint from passing
through. Thus if the gutta is not diluted
enough, the paint will just bleed through the
gutta and ruin your painting.

Achieving the right consistency of the gutta
is one of the hardest things to do when you
first take up silk painting. It took me a long
time to be able to get it right most of the time.

Until you are very familiar with the right
dilution, it is helpful to do your diluting
slowly, using small amounts of spirit at a time.
It helps to transfer some gutta to a smaller
container, or even to do the diluting in the
applicator pen. This will ensure that you do
not over-dilute your whole supply of gutta,
and have to wait for it to evaporate down to a
useable consistency. The process of
evaporation can take a day or so unless you
have a warm sunny spot in which to sit the
solution to hurry things along.

The gutta should be the consistency of
heated-up (runny) honey. If you have the right
dilution, the gutta should not run out without
your squeezing the pen a little, but you should
not have to squeeze very hard at all to make a
solid line of gutta appear on the silk. If you do
your diluting in the pen, then you can easily
test the consistency of the gutta mix (see 'Test
and Practice – All Guttas', steps 1 - 6, below).

Remember that thicker silks will need a
thinner dilution of gutta and possibly a nib
with a larger hole (for example a size 8).

To dilute spirit-based gutta and fill the pen:
◆ 1. Pour about 2 cm (1 in) of gutta into the
applicator pen, through a small funnel if you
are concerned not to spill it.
◆ 2. Use an eye-dropper to add about 1 cm
(¹/₂ in) of spirit.
◆ 3. Shake the pen vigorously (remember to
put your thumb over the hole, so you do not

get gutta decorating the ceiling, something I've done on occasion!).

◆ 4. Repeat this process until the pen is full.

◆ 5. Screw the nozzle onto the pen.

◆ 6. If you are using a new applicator pen, you will probably need to shave small pieces off the tip of the nozzle to make the nib fit. You will also need to cut off the end of the nozzle, just enough to make sure that the hole is open.

◆ 7. Push or screw the nib (depending on the type of nib you have) onto the end of the nozzle.

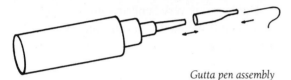

Gutta pen assembly

◆ 8. Seal the nib onto the nozzle with masking tape. Make sure that it is tightly fitted so that gutta does not leak out around the join.

◆ 9. Remove the wire from the nib and put it in a safe place.

WATER-BASED GUTTA

These guttas generally need less dilution than the spirit-based ones, as they have a much slower evaporation rate. Most can be used straight from the bottle without dilution, for quite long intervals.

Water-based guttas are harder to use than spirit-based ones as they tend to bubble and squirt. They can be made easier by adding about 1 cm ($^{1}/_{2}$ in) of spirit-based gutta to the mix as you are filling up the gutta pen, and shaking long and vigorously to get these two incompatible substances to mix. Bubbling and clogging can be minimised by pouring the gutta through a small wire sieve or tea-strainer into a funnel inserted into the gutta pen. Tapping the pen gently on the tabletop before you put the lid on can also help to get rid of air bubbles.

To dilute water-based gutta and fill the pen:
1. Follow steps 1 - 9 above, except that at step

1., pour the gutta through a small wire sieve or tea-strainer, as well as through a funnel.

◆ 2. Add 1 cm ($^{1}/_{2}$ in) spirit-based gutta, not plain spirit, to the pen. Do this without using an eye-dropper, as the gutta would clog the dropper.

◆ 3. Fill the rest of the pen 1 cm ($^{1}/_{2}$ in) at a time, using water-based gutta only (not spirit or spirit-based gutta), remembering to shake vigorously after each addition of gutta.

TEST AND PRACTICE – ALL GUTTAS

It is a good idea to test the dilution of the gutta first, and get a bit of practice, by drawing on a test piece of silk stretched on a small frame, or by drawing on the silk edges overlapping your frame which will be cut off later. Your aim is to make the lines as thin as possible without being so fine that the paint runs through.

◆ 1. Hold the pen the same way as you would hold a pencil. Hold it in the middle of the pen where the sides are softest, so that you are not trying to squeeze on the hard ridge.

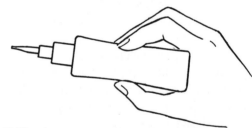

Holding the gutta pen

◆ 2. If gutta runs from the pen without you squeezing it, pour some of the mixture back into the bottle and add more undiluted gutta to the applicator, to thicken the mix.

◆ 3. Squeeze the applicator pen very gently and draw a line along the silk. Draw slowly and smoothly. The faster you draw the more likely it is that the lines will be too thin. Do not press down hard as this will tear or catch the silk: to get a more definite or thicker line you squeeze in on the pen, and draw more slowly. You barely need to touch the surface of the silk. Do not use back-and-forth sketching motions as you would with a pencil unless you go back and ensure that the sketchy lines meet up to form a barrier.

✦ 4. If the nib catches on the silk without your pressing down, then the nib may be rough. In this case, file it smooth with the metal nailfile.

✦ 5. If you have to squeeze hard on the pen to get the gutta to come out, so that your hand gets tired, the mix is too thick. You will need to pour some back into the gutta bottle to make room for more spirit, or more water in the case of water-based guttas. Test and re-mix until you have a workable gutta solution.

✦ 6. If your gutta makes blobs, the mix may be too dilute, or you may be using too big a nib. If it still blobs after you have changed these things, and it often does at the start of a line even with a perfect dilution, start the line on a piece of paper and draw off it onto the silk.

DRAWING A BORDER

You can do the border freehand, which is easier but unlikely to result in a straight line if you are new to gutta work, particularly as there is a need to draw slowly. Make a virtue of your shaky hand and let it curve and zigzag into a pattern.

To achieve a straight border:

✦ 1. Start with the side of the silk closest to you, and turn the frame around as you go to make access to each side easier.

✦ 2. To make sure your border meets at the

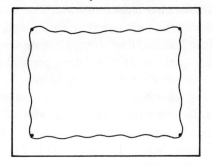

A shaky border

corners, instead of crossing, measure your chosen distance in from each side and make a little mark on the silk at the point where the two imaginary lines would join.

✦ 3. Measure and mark all four corners.

✦ 4. Place a large ruler against these marks, parallel to the edge of the frame, and hold it firmly in place.

✦ 5. Rest your pen against the ruler so that the nib is leaning outwards and touching the silk about 0.5 cm (¼ in) away from the ruler. This will stop the gutta from travelling under the ruler and smearing.

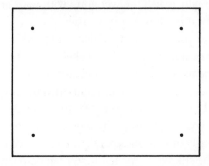

Measure and mark corners

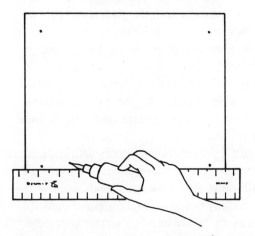

Using a ruler

✦ 6. Start from a corner, and draw a line to the mark in from the next corner. Try to draw the whole line along one side without taking your pen off the silk. It is surprisingly hard to do this, so do not worry if you cannot manage it at this stage: just make sure that you restart your gutta line so that there is no gap where you left off.

✦ 7. Turn the frame around, replace the ruler and draw the line from the corner you just reached, to the point in from the next corner.

✦ 8. Repeat until all sides have a border.

✦ 9. Check that there are no gaps where the corners meet.

DRAWING YOUR DESIGN

In general it is best to start drawing at the top of the silk, on the part which is furthest away from you, and work down, so that you do not accidentally brush the wet gutta with your arm and smear it. However it is easier to draw closer to you, so if you are using an abstract design or tracing a prepared sketch which can be done upside-down or sideways, work on the side nearest to you and then turn the frame around to provide easier access to each side.

✦ 1. If you are tracing from a design you have previously drawn onto paper you can trace it onto the silk with a pencil first, then go over it with gutta. This can be tedious, and you can trace it directly with the gutta if you like. In either case, place the drawing underneath the silk, close enough to see the design through the silk. Prop the drawing to be traced up at this level with books underneath it or, if you are going to be turning the frame around as you draw, loosely tape the design to the back of the silk.

Note: If you are tracing directly with gutta, make sure that the paper design does not touch the silk at the point where you are drawing, or the gutta may run or smear if the paper shifts. Similarly, be careful when you are taking the paper out: it is best to lift the frame straight upwards off the paper so that you do not slide one surface across the other and thus smear the gutta.

✦ 2. Draw the design onto the silk. Refer to 'Test and Practice' steps 1 - 6, above, for hints about achieving a good gutta line.

✦ 3. Let the gutta dry before applying the paint. Spirit-based gutta does not have to be totally dry but if properly diluted it should only take a few minutes. Water-based gutta will take half an hour or more. If you are in a hurry, dry it with a hair dryer.

Note: Make sure you do not hold the hair dryer too close to the silk, or over one spot for too long, as you could scorch the silk.

✦ 4. Once dry, water-based gutta may need to be ironed before it will hold the paint (refer to the manufacturer's instructions). If so, turn the frame upside down and iron the silk on the wrong side.

CHECKING AND REPAIRING GUTTA LINES

✦ 1. Check your gutta lines for gaps and thin bits and repair these before painting. Air bubbles do not matter, unless they clearly result in a gap in the line. Be sure to check every spot where two lines meet and make sure they actually join without a gap of even the smallest dimensions: the paint will bleed through the tiniest hole.

✦ 2. Repair thin lines and gaps by drawing more gutta over the top. If in doubt, add more gutta to a line. It is better to have a thicker line than to watch the paint bleed through and be unable to stop it.

✦ 3. Test any lines you are not sure of by applying clean water with a paintbrush inside the gutta line and seeing if it seeps out. Apply a lot of water, because the line may hold for a small amount, but break down with a lot. Gutta sometimes only survives painting on one side of the line, and then allows bleeding when you paint on the other side of it, so using a lot of water to test is helpful in spotting this.

✦ 4. If any water bleeds through, you must dry the wet silk before repairing the gap with more gutta, because gutta will not penetrate wet silk, and therefore there will be no barrier to the paint bleeding underneath the gutta line.

Again, use a hair dryer if you are in a hurry.

✦ 5. If you apply too much gutta, or put it in the wrong place, it cannot really be fixed up. For spirit-based gutta, you can rub the area with white spirit or Shellite and remove some of it that way, but a thin film will remain on the silk and show up as a white or pale area when painted. Water-based guttas will only smear when wet, and be totally immovable if dry.

It is best to try to make the mistake into an element of the design by turning it into a shape you can colour in ... or ignore it.

CLEANING THE PEN AND NIB

At the end of each day's silk painting it is advisable to return the gutta to the bottle, and to clean out the pen and nib. This will help to avoid unnecessary evaporation of the gutta, and clogging of the nib.

If you do leave your gutta in the applicator, make sure you insert the wire or pin in the nib so that it does not clog. There is less evap-oration with water-based gutta, but even so you should ensure that your pen is completely refilled at the end of each session, so that air in the pen does not lead to the gutta drying and flaking in the top half of the pen, thus causing small lumps which can clog the nib.

✦ 1. Remove the nib from the nozzle and clean it out with the aid of cotton buds and pipe-cleaners dipped in Shellite or white spirit for spirit-based guttas, or water for water-based guttas.

✦ 2. Re-insert the wire or pin.

✦ 3. Store the nib in a jar of Shellite or white spirit if you have been using spirit-based gutta, or in a dry place for either type.

✦ 4. Unscrew the nozzle from the body of the pen and empty the gutta back into the gutta bottle.

✦ 5. Clean out the nozzle and pen body using the small bottlebrush, cotton buds and pipe-cleaner dipped in spirit for spirit-based gutta, or water for water-based gutta. You may find it

necessary to soak the nozzle and pen body in the appropriate solution (spirit or water) if there is a stubborn residue of gutta.

✦ 6. Allow them to dry, and then store them in a dry place.

VARIATIONS

Paint coloured gutta on as a decoration using a paintbrush. This can be done before or after painting with the silk paints.

✦ Use water-based metallic gutta in an applicator pen to decorate painted silk, either when it is wet so that the gutta lines spread and blur, or when it is dry.

✦ Colour clear water-based gutta by diluting it with silk paint instead of water.

✦ Use clear water-based gutta to make paler lines in the paint by drawing with it onto silk which has just been painted, and is still wet. *Note*: The preceding two variations work best with particular brands: see the section on 'Brand Names'.

✦ Use gutta like wax in a batik: paint a colour or colours onto the silk, let it dry, draw over it with clear gutta, then paint the silk with another colour or colours, either over the gutta lines or on both sides of them. A clearer result is achieved if you paint next to the lines rather than over them. When the gutta is removed, the first colour will show through where the gutta lines were.

✦ Use gutta as a highlighter, either before or after painting with the silk paints. This is more readily achieved with coloured gutta: if you try to do this with clear gutta, you will need to paint a new colour next to it or on both sides of it, for any effect to be seen.

✦ Stamp or print the gutta on with a rubber stamp or some other printing mechanism (see 'Chapter 12'). You may find it hard to get a clear unbroken line this way, so be prepared for a 'messy' effect, and lines which will allow the paint to bleed through.

✦

4

BASIC INSTRUCTIONS FOR PAINTING

As most of this book is devoted to very detailed guides to specific painting effects, this chapter provides information on basic painting techniques, and some hints about how to do the hard things, such as backgrounds.

Materials
+ cotton buds
+ disposable gloves or a good barrier cream
+ eye-dropper
+ gutta pen filled with the gutta according to the instructions in 'Chapter 3'
+ jars with lids, for paints, and a big one without, for water
+ paintbrushes, a selection of sizes, preferably one for each colour
+ rags or tissues or paper towels
+ silk on a frame, prepared according to the instructions in 'Chapter 2' and 'Chapter 3'
+ silk paints, in a selection of colours, including at least the three primary colours and black or dark brown.
+ silk scraps, or a test piece stretched on a small frame
+ small funnel
+ water

Note: If you are using powder dyes you will need the other ingredients which go with them, such as lyogen and acetic acid: see the instructions which come with the dyes.

Optional:
+ ethyl rubbing alcohol or methylated spirits, if you wish to mix alcohol with the water used to dilute your paints
+ one or two foambrushes, as referred to in 'Chapter 1'
+ old shirt, or old clothes
+ pencil and paper
+ silk on a frame to use as a colour chart
+ sprayer
+ talcum powder, if you are using gloves

PROTECTION
Protect your hands from paint stains by putting on thin disposable gloves or a good barrier cream. If the gloves are hard to get on, put a little talcum powder in them first. Protect your clothes from paint stains, either by wearing old clothes, or by wearing an old shirt over your clothes.

COLOUR MIXING AND TESTING

Before you start a project, it is advisable to mix up the colours you will be using in the quantities needed, and to try out colour combinations and different levels of dilutions or colour mixtures on a scrap of silk. This can be your test piece from the previous chapter, or it can just be silk not on a frame.

If you will be painting a large area with one colour, or painting on a heavyweight silk, be sure to mix up enough of the colour to complete your project. It is almost impossible to get exactly the same hue if you run out halfway through.

Remember that if you are using chemical fixative alone, the colours will end up much paler than when you first paint them, so you will need to make them stronger than you actually want them to be.

Similarly, you will need to allow for the fact that the paint is much darker when it is wet than dry, so let the test piece dry before you decide on the colour dilutions. If you are in a hurry dry it with a hair dryer.

Note: If using a hair dryer to dry paint on your final product, be careful to move it continuously over a large area of silk. If you hold it still you will dry one area of paint while the other remains wet and you will get a watermark.

The range of colours you have to start with will depend on the brand you are using and, of course, the number of colours you have bought from that range. You can mix all possible colours from the three primary colours and black or dark brown, but the pre-mixed colours that are available save a lot of effort. There is no white: to get white areas on the silk you do not paint those spaces.

To get lighter colours you dilute the paint with water, or water and alcohol mixed 50:50. In fact, the manufacturers suggest that you should always use the paints diluted by at least 10 per cent, and preferably one third to a half, because there is more of a danger of the colours running during the fixing process if you use full strength (especially with black and red). If you want really vibrant colours, you can use them full strength, but I would only do this on small areas, and set the colour with steam before also using the chemical fixative.

If you dilute the paints too far by accident, and have no more pure paint, you can darken up areas by applying two or more coats, but watch out for watermarks formed by applying wet paint to a dry painted area.

If your paint has been sitting on the shelf for a long time and has sediment which does not mix in with shaking, warm it a little in the microwave on low for about 30 seconds.

It helps to make a colour chart for future reference. Use a piece of silk marked off into squares with gutta lines, and paint a square of each of the colours you like.

◆ 1. Start with the colours straight from the bottle or, if you are using powder dyes, mix the primary colours up according to the instructions.

◆ 2. Pour some of your base colour into a jar. The base colour is any colour which will form the main ingredient in your colour mix (for example, yellow if you want any variation of yellow, such as mandarine orange, lime green, golds, pale browns and so on).

◆ 3. When mixing or diluting your colours, add a little water, water/alcohol mix, or colour to your base colour at a time. Use an eye-dropper if you are mixing small amounts.

◆ 5. Test each mix or dilution on your test piece.

◆ 6. When you arrive at a colour you want to use, make a note either on your silk colour chart if you are making one, or on paper, of the proportions in the mix. It is surprising how easy it is to forget exactly what you have done to achieve a particular colour. If you are using paper to record the colour mixes, you can paint the colour directly onto the paper, and write the proportions next to it.

✦ 7. Having reached a colour you like, mix enough of it to use on your current project, or more if you think you will use it again.

✦ 8. Put the lid back on the jar until you are ready to use the paint.

✦ 9. Repeat the process until you have all the colours you want.

BASIC BRUSH WORK

✦ 1. Hold your brush as you would hold a pencil.

✦ 2. Dip your brush in the paint and let it soak up a lot of paint.

✦ 3. Wipe it gently on the side of the jar a few times so that it does not drip. It is better to dip your brush more often, than to take up so much paint in one go that it drops onto your silk in the wrong places. However, do not leave so little paint on the brush that you get streaks. It will take some practice to make this an automatic process.

✦ 4. While painting with one colour, dip your brush only into the paint, not into water, as this would dilute the paint and cause streaks.

✦ 5. Wash your brush thoroughly in clean water between colours. If this is not done properly, the last colour you used will come out onto the silk and cause muddy streaks. A good alternative is to use one brush for each colour: this conserves paint as well as ensuring clear colour.

✦ 6. Leave the border to paint last. This means that you can rest your arm on the frame to steady your hand as you paint, without getting paint marks on your arm.

✦ 7. Start by painting the lightest colours, so that if the paint bleeds through or goes over the gutta lines, you can cover the mistakes with darker paint.

✦ 8. Begin with the areas closest to you, and turn the frame around to reach the others, unless you are painting a picture which you

find hard to do upside-down and sideways. *Note*: Do not tilt the frame as you turn it if you have very wet paint on it. The paint can run over the edges of the gutta if you do this.

✦ 9. Paint one area at a time, and use a large brush for larger areas, and a small brush for smaller areas.

✦ 10. Do not have too much paint on your brush, or it may flood onto an area and cross the gutta line. If you find you have painted too much paint into a small area, wipe the excess off carefully with the corner of a tissue, rag, or cotton bud.

Note: The more paint you have in an area the darker the colour will be.

✦ 11. Place your brush in the middle of an area rather than close to the gutta lines.

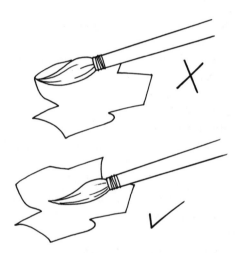

Place the brush in the middle of an area

✦ 12. Do not press down hard: let the paint do the work for you. One of the most satisfying qualities of silk paint is that you just need to touch the silk with your brush and the paint will travel across the fibres to fill in the corners for you. This generally means that you may not need to paint too close to the gutta. In fact, it is a good idea not to do so, because it is very easy to go over the line and paint will rapidly spread where you do not want it to be.

✦ 13. Paint in smooth, slow strokes, suiting the length of the stroke to the size of the space. For example, with a very small area you may just need to touch the silk with your brush in one spot in the middle, and let the paint run to all the edges, whereas you will need to run the brush over a larger space.

✦ 14. Add each new brushful of paint right next to the last one on the silk. Do not leave big gaps between, as it is harder to make the two blend together if you do.

✦ 15. Blend new paint into the last painted area with plenty of brush strokes.

SIMPLE BLENDING

✦ 1. To get two colours to blend, paint the second one next to the first before the first has begun to dry. The drier the first colour the harder it is to blend, and the more likely it is that you will get a hard edge forming.

✦ 2. Gently rub the brush over the area where the two colours meet, for a smooth transition.

✦ 3. If you need to, add more paint, of either of the two colours, to smooth out the blended area. Do not use water, as this will make it streaky.

✦ 4. If you are getting too much paint on the area and it is still not blended to your satisfaction, clean your paintbrush in the water jar, and squeeze out excess water. Use this dry brush to continue blending.

AVOIDING SPLATTERING

To avoid splattering make sure that you do not have too much paint on your brush. Paint with the tip of your brush rather than the side, and do not press too hard. Be careful when lifting your brush off the silk.

Unlike other paints you may be used to, such as acrylics, oils and gouache, silk paints are very watery, and it takes very little pressure for the paint to transfer to the silk.

If you do splatter the paint:

✦1. Immediately immerse a cotton bud in clean water and use it to scrub the paint away. The longer you leave it the drier the blob will be, and the harder to remove: this can take only seconds.

✦ 2. Use the dry end of the bud to partially dry off the wet silk.

Note: If the splatter landed on a part of your silk which was already painted, it is difficult to remove the blotch in this way without also fading the paint underneath it. You may decide to paint over the whole area again, or to turn your splatter into a part of the design if you can, by making a gutta shape around it (not on it, if it is still wet!).

GUTTA GAPS AND BLEEDS

If colour runs over or under the line, or through a gap, wash it off immediately with a cotton bud as for 'Avoiding Splattering' steps 1 - 2.

If the problem was caused by a gap in the gutta line, wait for the silk to dry (or use a hair dryer) before repairing the line.

Do not paint again on either side of the gap until you have repaired the gutta line, as paint will bleed back through the hole in the line. Note: Bleeds are the worst problem to deal with because when you scrub with the cotton bud, water bleeds through the gap and onto the area you have painted, thus fading it. At the same time, paint will continue to bleed out of the gap onto the unpainted area. The best solution is in fact prevention: check the gutta lines very carefully before you paint (see 'Chapter 3' 'Checking and Repairing Gutta Lines', steps 1 - 5).

LARGE AREAS AND BACKGROUNDS

The important thing to remember is that whenever wet paint meets dry paint, a watermark will form. If you do not want this to happen:

✦ Paint as quickly as you can without going over the lines. With practice, it is possible to paint very quickly, but to start with it is better to go a little more slowly so that you stay within the lines.

✦ Use a large brush with plenty of paint on it – or a foambrush – and if necessary change to a smaller paintbrush close to the gutta design.

✦ Start from a corner or edge within each gutta shape. Keep painting away from that beginning point. Paint across the shape, not along it. Work from the wet edge out.

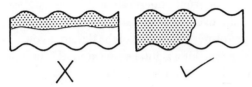

Paint across the shape, not along it

✦ Do not go back with wet paint to touch up a dry area unless you are then willing to go back over the whole area, painting it all again. If you want a smoothly painted colour with no evident brush stokes, and you cannot work quickly enough to achieve this the first time, paint a first coat and let it dry. Then go over the whole area again with the same colour. This second coat will intensify the colour, but it will also smooth out patchy areas.

Let the background colour dry before you paint the areas inside your design.

Covering the fabric with paint

You can paint the whole piece of silk with a pale background colour, either before or after you gutta it. The silk underneath the gutta will remain the colour of the paint, so that you will get coloured lines. Similarly, all of the colours you paint over the background colour will be changed by the presence of that colour on the silk, so that on a yellow background blue will become green, and so on.

This means that you cannot use very intense or dark colours on these types of background because the colours you paint over the top of it will not show up.

Covering the whole piece of fabric can be done either by immersing the silk in a bath of

the paint or dye, or by spraying it on the frame with paint in a sprayer (such as an empty laundry stain-remover bottle) or by painting it with a large paintbrush or foambrush.

Let the background colour dry completely before you gutta it, if you have not already applied the gutta.

You can always accept a background which is streaky or mottled rather than a smooth wash of colour. You can even make a feature of it by dropping water on it with an eye-dropper, or by rock-salting it (see 'Chapter 6').

PAINTING YOUR BORDER

✦ 1. Use a large paintbrush or foambrush.

✦ 2. Start from one corner, and place your brush near the gutta line, but not so close that you are in danger of having paint run across it.

✦ 3. Paint quickly along one side.

✦ 4. From then on, work on the two leading edges of paint, so that both are kept wet, and you do not get watermarks. Add paint to one edge and paint more along that side, then dip your brush in the paint and add more paint to the other edge and work on that side until you need more paint, and so on.

✦ 5. Turn the frame around as you go, to make access to each side easier.

✦ 6. If your resultant border is not smooth, leave it to dry and then apply another coat.

When you have finished painting, let the silk stay on the frame until it is completely dry.

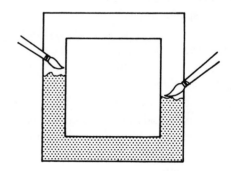

Keep the leading edges wet

5

Basic Instructions for Fixing

When you have finished painting your silk, you will need to fix or set the colour so that it is washable. The degree of colour fastness will depend on the type of paints or dyes you use, together with the method of setting.

While chemical fixing may be suggested as adequate for those paints which have such a fixative, I have found that you obtain a much better result by both steaming (either in a saucepan, pressure cooker, silk steamer or microwave) and chemical fixing. The colours remain more vibrant, the steam restores the lustre of the silk, and the combination of the two processes ensures a greater colour fastness.

Materials needed for each type of fixing are listed at the start of each of the appropriate sections below.

OPTIONS AND SPECIAL PRECAUTIONS

You will need to decide whether to set the colour by steaming, or by chemical fixative, or both. Another alternative is to take your silk to someone else to steam for you: ring your local Crafts Council or craft supplier to find out if there is anyone nearby who is providing this service.

If you decide to both steam and chemically fix your colours, you must steam first, or there is no point in steaming, as the fixative bath will wash out the extra colour you would have hoped to retain by steaming.

In all cases, it is best to let the silk rest for at least 24 hours between steaming and chemically fixing. This is because the heat opens up the fibres, and if you immerse the silk in liquid too soon after this, the dye will be more likely to run out again.

If you use a microwave to steam your colours, you must also use a chemical fixative: microwave steaming alone is not enough. This is probably the best method for doing one small-to-medium piece at a time, as there is less risk of creating watermarks, and creases do not get permanently set in the silk. (I *have* done 3 m (10 ft) pieces in the microwave, but there is more chance of getting watermarks the larger the parcel of silk you try to fit in.)

Steaming can also be done in the saucepan set or pressure cooker you may have in your home. These are good if you have only small amounts of silk to do. The silk steamer is for use with large quantities of silk: use it if you have saved your steaming until you have a lot to do.

Some techniques of silk painting require special care in steaming. Rock-salted silk should be steamed individually, or should be rolled up in such a way that each piece is placed well away from other pieces in the butcher paper if you are using a professional steamer. It is preferable to roll them in double sheets of paper. This is because the salt that inevitably remains in the silk absorbs water during steaming and some of the colour comes out, sometimes through the paper onto other silk, or even onto another part of the same silk. Double paper is not needed if you have used alcohol-based paints with the salt.

Similar precautions should be taken if you have been using strong dilutions of powder dye, as the sediment in the dye can transfer through one sheet of paper.

If you have been using the sugar syrup technique described in 'Chapter 10', double and sometimes even triple paper is recommended as the sugar solution can dissolve again in the steam.

PREPARING THE SILK

Drying can be done on or off the frame. The silk will need to sit for some time before you fix it if you are only using chemical fixative: up to 48 hours is recommended by some manufacturers. This is not really necessary if you are steaming or microwaving the silk prior to chemical fixing: in these cases you can go ahead soon after the paint is dry.

Make sure nothing wet gets near the silk before it is fixed because this will cause a watermark.

REMOVING GUTTA

You may want to rinse out clear spirit-based gutta if you feel the lines are too thick and sticky. Do not attempt to remove water-based gutta or coloured spirit-based gutta. The first will not come out; the second will dissolve but so will the gutta colourant, thus ruining your painting. Remove clear spirit-based gutta either before or after fixing the colour, as the spirit will not shift the paint or make it run.

Materials
+ large glass jar, or plastic bucket, with lid
+ Shellite or white spirit, 2 L (3½ pt)
+ rubber gloves or, better, industrial protective gloves

+ 1. Put gloves on before you put your hands in the spirit, as it will remove all the natural oils from your skin.
+ 2. Put about 2 L (3½ pt) of Shellite or white spirit in a large jar or bucket.
+ 3. Immerse the silk in the spirit. If you are using a bucket, scrub the silk as if you were washing it, concentrating on those parts where the gutta is thickest. If you are using a jar, put the lid on and shake vigorously.
+ 4. Leave it to sit for at least 10 minutes or as long as you like.
+ 5. Give the silk one final shake or scrub and rinse, then remove it from the spirit and wring it out.
+ 6. Hang it out to dry. It will dry in about 2 minutes, as long as you do not get any water near it.
+ 7. If any gutta still remains, repeat the whole process.

MICROWAVE OVEN STEAMER

Materials
+ absorbent kitchen paper (paper towelling)
+ plastic bag
+ scissors

✦ sharp implement to pierce the bag (for example, a wooden skewer)

✦ microwave oven

✦ microwave-safe bowl, of a size such that the colander will sit in the top of it, suspended about 4 cm (2 in) above the bottom of the bowl

✦ microwave-safe colander, of a size such that it will fit into the top of the bowl as above (the combined height of bowl and colander must fit in the microwave oven)

✦ water, enough to put 3 cm (1½ in) in the bottom of the bowl

✦ white vinegar, 1 tablespoon

Caution: If your microwave is also a convection oven, and you plan to use this method often (several times a week), make sure the machine is placed well away from walls so the vinegary steam can ventilate properly – otherwise the mechanism can corrode.

I have only tested this method with some brands of paints (see 'Brand Names'). If you want to try it with other types of paints and dyes, experiment first with a sample piece of painted silk.

You must check whether your particular type of microwave is capable of bringing the water to the boil quickly, and keeping it boiling. I tried this method in an old microwave, and kept on burning or scorching piece after piece of silk. Make sure that the water has already boiled, and that the oven has steam in it, before you place the silk inside. You must also be sure that your oven is capable of making the water boil again within a few seconds: even a wait of 30 seconds may be too long.

✦ 1. Wrap the silk in absorbent kitchen paper, with overlaps all round so you can make sure the paper covers all the silk. There is no need to lay the silk out flat unless there is sticky coloured gutta on it.

✦ 2. If you have sticky coloured gutta on your silk, it is worthwhile placing the silk on paper which is larger than the silk, and covering it with another piece of similar-size paper, then folding it all up so that no part of the silk touches any other part. This will prevent the gutta from transferring from one area to another.

✦ 3. Make sure no silk is protruding from the parcel.

✦ 4. Cut off any long loose threads which may hang out from the paper: these can transfer water onto the silk, thus ruining your painting.

✦ 5. Place this silk parcel inside a plastic bag and tie a tight knot to seal the bag. Do not have too much air in the bag: squeeze out as much as possible before you tie the knot.

Microwaving silk

✦ 6. Make sure the seams of the bag do not end up resting on the bottom of the parcel.

✦ 7. Punch three or four holes in the top of the bag, to ensure it does not burst in the microwaving process.

Note: In this case the 'top' and the 'bottom' refer to those parts of the bag closest to (bottom) and furthest away from (top) the water, once you put the silk in the colander over the bowl of water (see below).

✦ 8. Put 3 cm (1½ in) of water in a microwave-safe bowl, with 1 tablespoon of white vinegar.

✦ 9. Microwave this mixture on high (don't put the silk parcel and colander in yet) until the water boils furiously and causes steam to appear on the oven door. This may take approximately 3 minutes.

Note: It is absolutely essential that the water reaches boiling point, and you can see steam, before you put the silk parcel into the oven. Make sure that there is no delay between boiling the water and placing the silk parcel in the oven, so that the temperature remains close to boiling.

✦ 10. Place the silk parcel in a plastic colander and suspend it well above the water-level. The colander needs to fit into the bowl in such a way that it remains at least 2 cm (1 in) above the water in the bowl, so that water does not splash up onto the parcel.

✦ 11. Microwave on high for 8 minutes.

✦ 12. Immediately remove the silk from the oven and unwrap the parcel.

✦ 13. Let the silk rest for at least 24 hours before fixing the colour with the chemical fixative, following steps 1 - 4, 'Chemical Fixative', (page 47)

PRESSURE COOKER OR SAUCEPAN STEAMER

Materials

✦ aluminium foil
✦ butcher paper or paper towelling
✦ cake rack, vegetable basket or other wire mesh (see step 7 below)
✦ pressure cooker or saucepan
✦ water
✦ white vinegar, 1 tablespoon

✦ 1. Place the silk on a piece of butcher paper or enough absorbent kitchen paper (paper towelling) so that the paper is at least 1 cm (½ in) larger than the silk.

✦ 2. Cover the silk with more paper the same size as the first.

✦ 3. Make sure no silk is protruding.

✦ 4. Cut off any long loose threads which may hang out of the paper: these can transfer water onto the silk, thus ruining your painting.

✦ 5. Roll the silk and paper into a small parcel and seal the ends tightly with aluminium foil.

✦ 6. Put about 2 cm (1 in) of water, mixed with a tablespoon of vinegar, in your saucepan or pressure cooker.

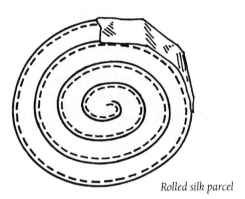

Rolled silk parcel

✦ 7. Place a cake rack, vegetable basket or other wire-mesh stand in the bottom of the receptacle. This improvised 'tripod' must clear the water by at least 2 cm (1 in) so that boiling water does not splash up onto the silk parcel. It is important that the parcel rests only on a few strands of wire rather than a flat surface with few or no holes, so that no water condensation can gather at the base of the silk roll.

Another way of doing this is to roll some aluminium foil into a cylinder, squash it flat, roll this into a spiral, and rest the parcel on that. Again, the height of the foil roll must be well above the water-level. Keeping the silk parcel away from water is essential, as any water which touches the paper will soak through onto the silk and mark it.

✦ 8. Put a cover of aluminium foil over the top of the silk parcel, folding the foil down over the parcel so that it forms a roof which will allow the condensation water droplets to roll off without touching the silk. Do not seal this aluminium around the silk: place it loosely over the top of the parcel so that there is a free flow of steam around the silk, but angle the edges of the foil away from the parcel so that the droplets of water condensation are directed away from the silk and paper roll.

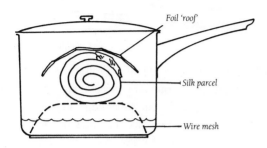

Steaming in pressure cooker or saucepan

◆ 9. Put the lid on your saucepan or pressure cooker.

◆ 10. If using a pressure cooker, steam the silk for 45 minutes to 1 hour.

◆ 11. If using a saucepan, steam for about 2 hours.

Note: Start the timing from when the water boils.

◆ 12. Keep an eye on the water-level, making sure it does not boil dry. I found out the hard way that if this happens, the silk will burn. Do not keep taking the lid off to check: take note of whether or not steam is escaping from your container and only interrupt the steaming process if you are fairly sure that there is no water left.

◆ 13. Remove the silk from the steamer as soon as the time is up.

COMMERCIAL-SIZE STEAMER: STOVE-TOP AND UPRIGHT

Materials
◆ roll of butcher paper at least 1 cm (½ in) wider than your widest piece of silk
◆ length of dowelling to fit across tripod notches in stove-top; or steamer rod and 'tripod' fixtures which come with the upright steamer
◆ masking tape
◆ scissors
◆ steamer
◆ water

◆ 1. Choose butcher paper that is wider than the silk, but not as wide as your dowelling (for stove-top steamers) or steamer rod (for upright steamers).

◆ 2. You need room to roll up a reasonable length of silk and butcher paper at a time – either a workbench surface at least 2 m (6 ft) long, or the floor.

◆ 3. Unroll about 2 m (6 ft) of butcher paper and start to roll this very tightly onto the dowelling (stove-top) or steamer rod (upright). Roll at least 1 m (3 ft) of paper onto the dowelling or rod before starting on the silk.

◆ 4. Lay your silk out onto the paper that is still spread out, leaving at least 1 cm (½ in) of space clear at the edges of the paper. Leave plenty of space between each successive piece of silk (enough to ensure a complete turn of the silk-filled roll so that there is a layer of paper between silks). Make sure that no piece of silk touches any other silk next to it. Both of these precautions are necessary because the colour can be transferred from one piece of silk to the other if there is not enough paper or space between them.

◆ 5. Make sure no silk and no threads are protruding over the edges of the paper: re-roll

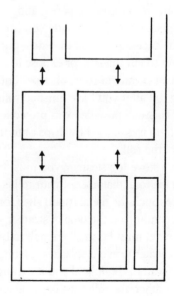

Laying silk out on the paper

if edges emerge, and cut off any threads before rolling the silk. Either of these can soak up water and bring it inside the roll, to ruin your silk painting.

✦ 6. Roll the paper and silk onto the dowelling or steamer rod, being careful not to crease the silk as you go, as these creases will be permanently pressed into the silk by the steaming.

✦ 7. Keep the paper rolling straight by placing it parallel to the table edge (or to the wall or some other straight line if you are doing it on the floor) every time you roll out more paper. You will need to continually push the ends of the cylinder of paper in towards the middle of the dowelling or rod to keep the roll straight.

Push the ends in as you go

This is quite difficult to do, and you will need to hold the roll of paper-wrapped silk firmly in one hand while you push the wayward paper back in with the other. If you do not do this you will end up with an ever-widening roll which turns into a cone of paper, and will not fit in your steamer. If desperate, you can cut or tear the excess paper off the ends, but be careful not to cut the silk, or expose it.

✦ 8. Roll an extra 2 m (6 ft) of paper onto the steaming roll after you have finished rolling all the silk. This will provide extra protection from watermarks caused by drips onto the outside of the roll.

Note: For a stove-top steamer, you must make sure that the total diameter of your roll is not so large as to touch the metal tripod shelf, or the water, depending on the type of steamer you have. The roll must be small enough to be well above the water to avoid splashes reaching it when the water is boiling. If you are using an upright steamer, the roll must be small enough not to touch the sides of the steamer.

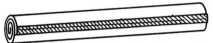

Use one piece of tape

✦ 9. Cut the paper and seal the roll well with masking tape. Use one long piece of tape to seal completely along the cut paper edge. I have found that joining two pieces of tape into a double layer can cause water to collect and soak through onto the silk. Do not seal the cylinder ends, as it is best to have the maximum flow of steam through the silk and paper roll.

✦ 10. Put 2 cm (1 in) of water or more, depending on the depth of your steamer, in the bottom of the stove-top steamer, or a maximum of 2 L (3½ pt) in the upright steamer.

✦ 11 (a). In the stove-top, place the ends of the dowelling in the notches of the tripod, to suspend the silk and paper roll over the water. Do not let the cylinder of paper-covered silk touch the bottom of the stand or the sides of the tripods. Make sure it is suspended well above the water.

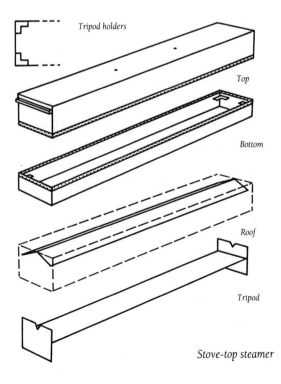

Tripod holders

Top

Bottom

Roof

Tripod

Stove-top steamer

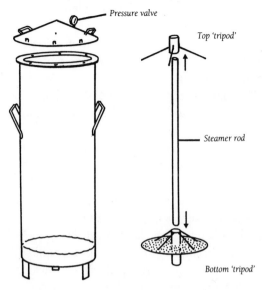

Upright steamer

✦ 11 (b). In the upright steamer, place your steamer rod in the bottom metal 'tripod' holder, and secure it with a nail. Place this in the steamer without tipping it over too far because the water that you have already placed in the cylinder could wet the silk and paper roll. Put the top metal 'tripod' holder onto the steamer rod.

Note: The combined height of the upright steamer and the silk and paper roll will require you to stand on a chair, steps or a ladder to insert the roll into the steamer. So there will be a limited number of places where you can do your steaming, as it is not wise to move the water-filled steamer once you have placed the silk in it.

✦ 12. Place the lid on your steamer and bring the water to the boil. In the case of the upright steamer of the pressure-cooker type illustrated in this book, you will need to release the pressure safety valve a few times during the heating-up process to bleed off cold air. Every time you do this, feel the air current so released. When hot steam rather than cool air is released, it is time to leave the pressure weights on to bring the pressure up. As soon

as the safety valve begins to hiss loudly, turn the gas down and let the water in the steamer return to simmering, signalled by a regular but quiet hissing

✦ 13. Steam for up to $1\frac{1}{2}$ or 2 hours, depending on the thickness of your roll of silk and the dyes you are using (refer to the instructions which come with the paints or dyes). If your steamer is a pressure-cooker type, the time can be shorter: refer to the manufacturer's instructions.

CHEMICAL FIXATIVE

Materials
✦ chemical fixative
✦ coffee filters
✦ flat wide container, e.g. plastic type
✦ gloves, thin disposable, or rubber kitchen type
✦ sealable container, any type
✦ water

Before chemically fixing, leave the silk to stand for at least 48 hours after painting if you have not microwaved or steamed it, or for 24 hours after microwaving or steaming, to allow the fibres to rest.

Use the chemical fixative which goes with the paints or dyes you are using. Do not expect a fixer which is designed for one set of dyes or paints to have any effect at all on any other type. Experiment if you like, and you may find there are chemicals which work across a range of paints and dyes, but do this experimenting on samples, not on precious pieces of painting!

✦ 1. Dilute the fixer according to the instructions on the bottle, putting the solution into a flat wide container if you have not steamed or microwaved the silk first. This is important if the paint has not already been stabilised by one of these processes, as colour can transfer from one surface to another if the silk is scrunched up to fit in a small container. The kitchen sink is about the right shape and size for a scarf, although an even bigger bottom surface area is better. The trouble with using a sink is that if you want to store the solution to use it again, it is hard to get it all out of the sink and into another container. *If you do use the kitchen sink, clean it thoroughly afterwards.*

✦ 2. Immerse the silk in the fixative bath. If the silk has not been steamed or microwaved first, try not to fold or squeeze it much, as the excess paint will be coming out as soon as the silk gets wet, and this can cause the colours to run. This is not an issue if the silk has been steamed or microwaved: in these cases it is a good idea to squeeze the fixative solution through the silk as if you were washing it.

✦ 3. Leave the silk to soak for as long as specified in the fixative instructions: for 5 minutes, or longer.

✦ 4. Agitate the silk in the bath from time to time, so that the fixer reaches all the silk evenly. *Note:* Some of the paint or dye will come out of the silk during this process of chemical fixing, no matter how much you have pre-pared the silk by steaming or microwaving first. The fixer may be used again provided that it is not too badly discoloured by excess dye or paint. Pour it into the sealable container through a coffee filter to take out as much of the colour as you can. If it is badly discoloured, throw it away.

INITIAL WASHING OF THE SILK

This can be done immediately after chemically fixing, or 24 hours after steaming.

✦ 1. Wash the silk by hand in cold water using a mild soap such as a wool wash. Never wash in warm or hot water, because in either case you will fade the colour. Some colour will continue to come out at this stage: this is excess paint or dye, and not a problem unless too much keeps pouring out of the fabric. If this happens, put it back in the fixer bath for a while.

✦ 2. Do not soak the silk because this will make some of the colour come out. Keep agitating and squeezing it.

✦ 3. Rinse in clear water with a tablespoonful of vinegar added.

✦ 4. If the rinse water has colour in it, repeat the wash and rinse processes until no more colour comes out.

✦ 5. Squeeze excess water out of the silk by rolling it in a towel and twisting until the silk has been wrung almost dry. If left to dry too slowly from saturation point, there is a danger that the colour will run. If you have squeezed out excess moisture this way you do not really need to hang the silk out, but can iron it dry. This is especially helpful if you are trying to dry the silk on a rainy day or using colours that are susceptible to running (for example silk that has not been steamed or microwaved, or silk painted red and black against a white background), and particularly if this is the first time the silk is being rinsed after fixing.

✦ 6. The first time you wash and dry the silk after fixing it is the most sensitive time, so keep an eye on the silk as it is drying. If it looks as if the colours are beginning to run, quickly take it off the line and immerse it in water again: if you can catch a colour run before it is quite dry, it is possible to wash out the offending colour. Once it has dried, the colour run will be permanent.

✦ 7. Take your silk off the line just before it is quite dry, so that you can iron it while it is still damp. The creases will not come out properly if you let the silk dry completely before ironing. Dampen it again if this occurs.

IRONING

Iron the silk while it is still quite damp or even wet. If really wet, squeeze it dry in a towel as above, then iron quickly over the whole surface rather than ironing one bit dry and then going on to the next because this can cause watermarks.

 Another way of preparing silk for ironing instead of wetting or dampening it is to put it in a plastic bag in the freezer for half an hour.

CARE OF THE SILK

Basically, all your fears about silk are from buying finished products (clothes in particular) which may not have been pre-shrunk, and may not have colour-fast dyes. It is actually very easy to care for silk which you have painted yourself, because you have already washed it and made it shrink as far as it can, and have fixed it so you know it is colour-fast.

Hand-wash according to the instructions above. You can machine-wash the silk, but thisis really only useful for large quantities which have been painted in similar colours, as you should do each colour set separately in case the colour comes out a bit and stains.

To remove stains made by water-based substances marking the silk, wash the whole item as above. If the stain is greasy, use white spirit. Carefully spot-clean if the item has coloured spirit-based gutta on it, as spirit can smear the gutta. If there is no gutta, or if there is water-based gutta, immerse the whole item in spirit. See 'Removing Gutta' steps 1 - 7 (page 42).

Store your silk in a cool dry drawer or wardrobe, away from sunlight, which can fade it.

6

WET AND DRY PAINT INTERACTIONS

Wet and dry paint interactions bring out some of the loveliest qualities of the silk paints. The ways in which they react on silk with each other, and with water, are different from any other kind of paint. You can create marvellous effects with very little effort, just by letting the natural properties of the paints work for you.

The techniques in this chapter are based on two main themes: what the paint can do when it is wet, and what can be done when it is dry. The distinction between the two is based on the fact that, when wet, the paint will run to form soft blendings and, when it is dry, any addition of liquid to it will form hard lines. In either case, we are relying on the paint's workability: until the colour is fixed it is possible to keep on 'working' it to change it.

Materials

✦ designs as for 'Chapter 2'
✦ thin disposable gloves or barrier cream
✦ paints or dyes, diluted and tested as described in 'Chapter 4', but note step 2 below
✦ paintbrushes, a selection of sizes including at least one large one, and preferably one large one for each colour

✦ rags, tissues or paper towelling
✦ silk on a frame, prepared according to instructions in 'Chapter 2', but note step 1 below
✦ water

Materials for Variations

✦ antifusant
✦ commercial diffusant, or lyogen: a few drops per colour
✦ cornflour
✦ cotton buds, cottonwool balls, toothbrushes and other household items
✦ ethyl rubbing alcohol, or methylated spirits (enough to dilute your colours when mixed 50:50 with water, and enough for spraying the silk)
✦ eye-droppers (preferably two)
✦ foambrush
✦ gutta pen filled with gutta as described in 'Chapter 3'
✦ hair dryer
✦ hard-bristled brush
✦ at least one packet of large-grained rock-salt
✦ table salt, and salts of various grain sizes (see below)

♦ sprayer

♦ teaspoons, one for each colour

♦ urea grains, about a cupful (available at craft suppliers and garden or pool suppliers)

ROCK-SALT TECHNIQUE

It is a good idea to start with this most simple, but very effective, method of playing with wet paint. Rock-salt thrown onto silk which has been covered with wet paint will cause a mottling not unlike some forms of marbling. See colour plates on pages 5 and 14.

The technique will work when the silk paints are diluted with water, but it is best not to use too dilute a mixture because the paler the colour, the less remarkable the effect.

The results you achieve will be more startling if you use alcohol-based paints, or the strongly pigmented powder dyes. You can make the ordinary silk paints alcohol-based by diluting them with a mixture of 50:50 alcohol and water, rather than just water. Another option is to add a few drops of diffusant or lyogen to each colour as you are mixing it up.

You can use grains of salt of any size, but the most interesting effect is achieved with very large grains.

♦ 1. Attach a piece of silk to the frame following steps 1 - 6, 'Attaching the Silk to the Frame' (page 28). Attach it more tightly than usual, with the staples or pins closer together, so that it does not sag with the wet paint and cause the salt to roll into the middle.

♦ 2. Following steps 1 - 8, 'Colour mixing and Testing' (page 37), mix up the colours you wish to use, but less diluted than usual as this method requires a more intense concentration of pigment to work well. Alternatively, dilute with a mixture of 50:50 alcohol and water, or add a few drops of lyogen or commercial diffusant to each colour.

Note: An effective set of base paints you might like to try is the colours of the rainbow. These are red, orange, yellow, green, light blue, dark blue, purple ... and hot pink for good measure.

♦ 3. Set the jars of paint out in the order you wish to use them, with the lids off, so you can work very quickly. Having colours which are close to each other on the spectrum close to each other on the silk works well, as they will blend into each other easily.

♦ 4. Using a large paintbrush with lots of paint on it, paint wide stripes of each colour from one side of the silk to the other. Remember, if you are only using one paintbrush, wash it between colours so as not to contaminate the next jar of paint. Squeeze out excess water before putting the brush into the next colour, so that you do not dilute the paint each time.

♦ 5. Quickly blend each successive colour into the one which went before. The aim is to finish with all the colours well blended but still wet.

Note: If you are using alcohol in the paints they will dry more quickly, but this is balanced by the fact that they do not need to be as wet as the water-based paints to work well.

♦ 6. If you take longer the first time and the first one or two colours are almost dry when you have finished laying down all the colours, go back and quickly add more paint to those stripes before going on to the next step.

♦ 7. Scatter the rock-salt evenly onto the silk by throwing it across the frame. This will mean that some goes onto the bench and the floor, but will allow a more even spread. Throwing the salt also helps to ensure that you do not get too much salt too close together on the silk, which results in lots of small dark dots of colour rather than the mottled effect.

Note: If the weather is humid, or the salt has soaked up moisture for any other reason, dry it out in the oven before using it.

♦ 8. Carefully drop more salt onto areas where there is none, but do not overdo it.

♦ 9. Allow the paint to dry completely before brushing the salt off.

♦ 10. When the silk is completely dry, remove

as much of the salt as possible. The wetter the silk was when you put the salt onto it and the smaller the grains of salt, the harder it will be to brush off. The more salt left on the silk the more it will soak up water during steaming, and possibly result in paint transferring through the paper onto other pieces of silk.

◆ 11. Store used rock-salt in a separate container from clean salt: it can be used again, but the paint already soaked up has a tendency to run back out again onto wet silk. If the salt is very wet, dry it on a tray in the oven before storage.

◆ 12. Remove the silk from the frame, leave it to rest, and then fix and wash as described in 'Chapter 5'.*Remember:* double paper in steaming.

Variations

◆ Use different sizes of salt.

◆ Cover the silk with a coat of antifusant before painting.

◆ Use grains of urea instead of rock-salt. The effect achieved is more strongly mottled, and the urea acts as a bleach, taking the colour right back to white under the grain, if you leave it on long enough.

◆ Apply rock-salt only to parts of a design.

◆ Apply the paint in shapes and patterns other than stripes.

◆ Use layers of colours, painting wet onto wet paint, or wet onto dry paint, painting one dark colour over several blended colours, or several colours over a layer of blended colours. Layering of paint in this manner creates more definite mottling. You can even paint a piece of silk, take it off the frame and fix the colour, and then follow steps 1 - 12 above to get a very strong mottling.

◆ Drop or spray paint, alcohol, water, or a weak solution of urea and water onto the painted silk either before or after rock-salting one layer of colour. Do this either before or after the first layer is dry, to get different effects.

◆ Drop well-used rock-salt onto silk that has

been wet all over with just water, so that the paint in the salt comes out onto the silk. This is a very pale effect.

◆ Remove the salt from the silk after it has dried, and then use the painted silk as a background: gutta and paint a design onto it. A border done in this way is very effective. In both cases you need to be careful to paint right up to the gutta lines, as the residual salt in the silk will draw the paint away from the lines.

◆ To paint a contrasting border, gutta the border line onto your silk before rock-salting it. Paint the middle section and rock-salt it as above, then carefully remove any grains of salt on the unpainted border, especially those which rest on the gutta lines as these will drag paint across the line onto the border. Paint the border last.

WET AGAINST DRY TECHNIQUE

A simple but very effective design can be made by just painting wet paint next to paint which has been allowed to dry, letting the second colour run into the first and form a hard wavy line.

◆ 1. Paint lines, shapes or patterns onto the silk, using only one colour. Use a small to medium-size brush, and leave large spaces between the areas of paint to accommodate the other colours.

◆ 2. Let this first colour dry completely. Use a hair dryer if you are in a hurry.

◆ 3. Paint another colour next to the first. Do not let your brush actually go over onto the first colour very much, if at all, because the second colour will bleed onto the first anyway.

◆ 4. Let the second colour dry.

◆ 5. Repeat this process until you have used all the colours you want, or until you have filled all the white spaces on the silk.

◆ 6. Allow the paint to dry completely before removing it from the frame.

◆ 7. Let the silk rest, and then fix the colours according to 'Chapter 5'.

Variations

✦ Paint lines, shapes, dots or other designs onto silk which has already been painted with colours and allowed to dry. Start by using a small brush with little paint on it, as this is easiest to control. See colour plate on page 14.

✦ Use an eye-dropper, or a brush, to paint small dots of paint onto the silk, all over an area but leaving spaces in between to put other colours. Lightly touch the eye-dropper to the silk and squeeze very gently, so that your dots do not get too big. Let the first colour dry and then do the same with another colour, placing the dots next to the first set of spots. Let that dry and repeat the process with different colours until the silk is completely covered.

✦ Use different sized brushes, and different amounts of paint on the brushes, to get varying effects.

✦ Use different implements to apply the paint: cotton buds, cottonwool balls, toothbrushes, or anything you can think of.

✦ Do not allow the first colour to dry completely before applying the second, and so on for each colour: you will find that varying levels of dryness will result in slightly different interactions of the paint.

✦ Dark outlines can be obtained within gutta shapes. Paint inside the shape, and let that dry. Then paint water, or another lighter colour, in the middle of the area, gradually moving to the sides of the gutta, or letting the paint or water run to the sides by itself if the area is small enough. The wet paint will push some of the pigment of the dry colour towards the gutta lines, so that the result is a fine dark line just inside the gutta, with a paler middle area. If you have a lot of paint or water on your brush for the second coat, you will get a wavy line of darker colour, rather than a straight one.

✦ Fold or pleat silk which has not been stretched on a frame. Spray this with a fine light spray of colour. Let that dry and then either spray another colour inside the folds, or move the folds or pleats and spray. Repeat this process until you have the effect you want.

WET ON WET TECHNIQUES AND VARIATIONS

All of the techniques so far discussed in the context of wet against dry paint can be used to make completely different results just by painting the colours in quick succession, without waiting for each to dry. You will find some very surprising reactions of the paints, for example lighter colours placed on top of darker colours will actually push the paint away, leaving a light patch in the middle of dark.

✦ Paint an area one colour, and while it is still damp, but not saturated, use a small brush to apply another colour in shapes or lines or dots over the top.

✦ Use a foambrush, cottonwool ball or large paintbrush to paint the whole silk with water, or with lighter shades of paint. Dry the silk slightly by absorbing the excess with a tissue or rag, and then paint a design on top of the wet silk. A very simple but effective result can be obtained by using a large stiff-bristled brush with very little paint on it, and pressing down hard so that the bristles splay apart as you paint, giving lots of parallel lines. This is similar to dry-brush technique in water-colour.

✦ Shading within a gutta shape can be obtained by painting inside the shape with one colour, either over the whole of the shape or in parts of it. While this is still damp, but not saturated, paint a second colour, or water, on it or next to it, and blend the two together with repeated brush strokes. An easy way to do this for complementary colours or shadings of one colour is to paint the whole area with the main colour you want. Before this dries, paint water or another lighter colour in the middle of the area, gradually moving to the sides, or letting the water or paint run to the sides if the area is small enough.

✦ Use an eye-dropper to apply different

coloured paints, and let them run into each other. Drop smallish drops of one colour all over the desired area, then quickly change to another colour and do the same, and so on until the silk is all filled up with colour. This can be done even more effectively by holding an eye-dropper in each hand, with a different colour in each, and dropping the two colours right next to each other as you go. You will achieve different results if you drop the colours next to each other or onto each other. The scarf illustrated on page 8 was painted with this technique, and then petals drawn on with a black fabric pen (see 'Chapter 14' for instructions on use of fabric pens).

✦ Spray one colour on top of another, while the first is wet. This works better with alcohol-based paints or with the powder dyes, but a good effect can be obtained with ordinary silk paints if your spray is fine enough.

✦ Apply large amounts of paint to the silk, in stripes or shapes, so that the silk is almost dripping. Tilt the frame so the colours run down the surface of the silk. Tilt the frame in another direction to do the same, until you have achieved the effect you want.

✦ Thicken the paints with cornflour, adding a little at a time and stirring thoroughly, until the paint is thick but still runny. Take a spoonful of thickened paint and hold it over the silk. Dribble or shake it onto the silk in lines or dots or patterns. Let this dry a little, and then paint unthickened paint of the same colour in some of the spaces between the lines, letting the paint run into the lines where it will. Do the same with the next colour, letting lines cross the first colour if desired. Repeat this process until you have used all the colours you want. Let this dry completely. Scrape off the dry cornflour before fixing the colour according to 'Chapter 5'.

PAINTING WITH WATER

After the first coat of paint, any of the techniques for wet against dry and wet on wet can be used substituting clean water for paint at any point. Again, different results will be achieved if the paint is allowed to dry before applying water, or is left wet or damp.

✦ The water will make very definite dark lines in the paint already on the silk if you dry the water with a hair dryer as soon as you apply it. This is particularly good for painting lines, dots, shapes and other patterning onto the painted silk to texturise the colour. For example, it is a simple way to create light and shade and texture in landscape paintings.

✦ Use an eye-dropper to drop clean water all over painted silk. A different effect will be obtained depending on whether you let the first coat of paint dry or not, and whether you have one or more layers of colour. For example, dropping water onto paint which has also been applied in dots by an eye-dropper will make a very swirly mottled or marbled effect. Applying water with an eye-dropper is best done in lots of little drops, touching the dropper to the silk and squeezing gently. Each drop should be placed close to the last one. Work quickly so the drops do not spread too far. You can enhance the effect by using a hair dryer to dry it after the whole silk has been dotted but before the drops get too big, or by following the eye-dropper with the hair dryer as you go. See colour plate on page 8.

✦ Sprinkle water onto painted silk by flicking a brush, shaking drops from your fingers, or spraying it with a coarse spray.

✦ Add a spoonful of diffusant or lyogen to the water.

✦ Add a spoonful of urea to the water, and dissolve it thoroughly.

✦ Add alcohol to the water, to make a 50:50 solution.

✦

7

ANTIFUSANT AND DIFFUSANT

This chapter contains information about two solutions which can be used (a) to negate the bleed (antifusant) or (b) to exaggerate the way fabric paint bleeds into and across the fabric (diffusant).

Antifusant is most often painted onto the silk before using the colours. It coats the silk with a thin layer of resist, not enough to prevent the paint from entering the fabric, but enough to stop it from bleeding. Thus painting over the antifusant is like painting water-colours on paper, and gutta lines are not needed to control the paint flow.

Antifusant is most commonly a solution of gutta and spirit: you can buy it ready-made or make your own. You will need to re-dilute this type of antifusant by adding more spirit if it has been left on the shelf too long. If it gets too strong, it becomes like gutta and will not let the paint into the silk.

A supersaturated solution of salt and water can be used instead, but the results are very different because the paint still bleeds a little, very unevenly, and small 'grains' of white silk shine through.

Diffusant, which makes the colour bleed further, can be added directly to the paint or dye, or it can be diluted with water and applied to the silk either before or after it is painted. You can buy commercial diffusants, made by the same companies which make the paints. In most cases, lyogen diluted with water can be used as a cheaper and equally effective substitute.

Materials
+ bucket or large jar of white spirit or Shellite, as in 'Chapter 5', for removing antifusant
+ commercial antifusant, up to 200 mL (8 fl oz); or to mix: 20 mL (0.8 fl oz) clear spirit-based gutta, and 180 mL (7 fl oz) white spirit or Shellite
+ commercial diffusant, or lyogen, up to 100 mL (4 fl oz) undiluted
+ cottonwool balls
+ designs as for 'Chapter 2', and 'Gum Blossom' design (see page 88)
+ thin disposable gloves, or barrier cream
+ rubber gloves or industrial safety type for removing antifusant
+ gutta pen filled according to directions in 'Chapter 3', with gold water-based gutta
+ paints or dyes diluted and tested according to directions in 'Chapter 4'
+ paintbrushes, a selection of sizes, preferably one for each colour

◆ pencil and eraser and, if available, a photocopier with enlarging capability
◆ pegs
◆ rags, tissues or paper towels
◆ silk prepared and stretched on a frame according to directions in 'Chapter 2'
◆ water

Materials for Variations
◆ antifusant made from equal parts salt and water, thoroughly mixed
◆ blotting paper, several small sheets
◆ cornflour, up to half a cupful, or carragem mixed as described in 'Chapter 12'
◆ cotton buds
◆ double-sided tape
◆ drinking straws, one for each colour
◆ eye-dropper
◆ fabric pens
◆hard-bristled brush
◆ masking tape
◆ paper, several sheets of letter or typing paper, not too absorbent and not too shiny
◆ salt: small grained table or cooking salt, and large grained rock-salt
◆ sprayer
◆ stencils: cutouts as in 'Chapter 12', leaves, plates, plastic or wire mesh, lace, sticks of uncooked spaghetti, rice, and other items
◆ teaspoons, one for each colour
◆ toothbrushes, hairbrushes, sponges, plastic food wrap

ANTIFUSANT TECHNIQUE
Silk covered with the gutta/spirit solution is the easiest and most effective use of antifusant. The 'Gum Blossom' scarf in the colour plate on page 10 has been painted in this way, without gutta. The 'Gum Blossom' scarf in the colour plate on page 13 has been painted by the serti method, with paints that bleed held in by gutta lines. There is quite a contrast between the two completely different effects using the same design!

Antifusant 'Gum Blossom' Scarf
◆1. Use commercial antifusant, or mix up a solution of 10 per cent gutta and 90 per cent white spirit or Shellite. Shake it well to mix it thoroughly and dissolve the gutta.
◆ 2. Use a peg to hold the cottonwool balls as you dip them in this mixture. Soak up a lot of antifusant.
◆ 3. Rub the cottonwool all over the silk, to coat it completely with a thin film of antifusant.
◆ 4. Let the silk dry completely. This should not take more than a few minutes.
◆ 5. Enlarge the 'Gum Blossom' design on page 89 on a photocopier, and then trace it onto the silk in pencil, or use a pencil to copy it directly onto the silk.
◆ 6. Paint a rough border in pink, using a small brush to make sketchy lines.
Note: For better control of the paint flow, use small to medium brushes throughout, and wipe the brush thoroughly on the side of the paint jar to ensure that the brush does not have a lot of paint on it. Wherever you paint one colour over another, the paint will run slightly and blend a little: too much paint will run where you do not want it to go. Use a hair dryer to dry it quickly, if need be.
◆ 7. Paint first grey and then fawn on the stems, gumnuts and branches.
◆ 8. Use dark brown to make the shadings on each.
◆ 9. Paint all the leaves a flat green-gold colour. Pencil lines will remain just visible but will disappear with washing.
◆ 10. Paint in the shadows and outlines in a dark green. Where you want these to blend, rub in the colour with gentle brush strokes. If desired, extra blending can be achieved by dipping the brush in water, squeezing it almost dry, and rubbing the paint on the silk with this.
◆ 11. Add some stippling of tiny dots of fawn to the lighter areas on the leaves.

✦ 12. Use a very fine brush to paint thin lines of pink, and then purple, for the flower stamens. For better separation of the stamens, let the pink dry a little before applying the purple.

✦ 13. Add dots of water-based gold gutta to the ends of the stamens, as the pollen granules. You must use water-based gutta, because spirit-based gutta will rinse out with the antifusant at step 15.

✦ 14. Allow the painting to dry completely before removing it from the frame.

✦ 15. Rinse the antifusant out in white spirit or Shellite, as for removing gutta in 'Chapter 5'.

✦ 16. Let the silk rest, and then fix the colour as per 'Chapter 5'.

Variations

Antifusant can be combined with many of the other techniques in this book. It is mentioned specifically in some chapters, for example 'Chapter 10' on sugar syrup and 'Chapter 12' on stencilling, but experiment with the other techniques as well, such as blending in 'Chapter 6'.

✦ In general, the antifusant is left to dry completely before paint is applied, but a different effect can be obtained by painting while it is still wet. You will need to wash your brushes in water, let them dry, and then clean them in white spirit at the end of the session if you do this.

✦ Paint the silk with pale background colours, or do a border, before covering it with antifusant. Remember that any colour in the background will change the colours you paint over it.

✦ You can paint a whole design in a wash of watercolour techniques, let it dry, cover the painting with antifusant, and then add details and highlights without fear that this layer of paint will run too far. You can do this over a gutta design too, but it must be clear spirit-based or water-based gutta, because the antifusant would smear coloured spirit-based gutta.

✦ Use a salt solution instead of diluted gutta as the antifusant. In this case the antifusant cannot be rinsed out until after the colour has been fixed, as it requires water, not spirit, to remove the salt. If you want to use gutta to make borders or designs over the top of salt-soaked silk, you will need to carefully paint right up to the gutta lines, and even then the salt will prevent the paint from settling evenly.

✦ Use a hard-bristled brush, or cotton bud, to paint the antifusant onto the silk in patterns, or only on parts of it. The result will be colours which run and blend on those parts of the silk which have not been treated, and which stay pure and separate on the areas which have been coated. See colour plate on page 7.

✦ Place a large drop of paint onto silk which has been coated with antifusant. Blow at the paint through a drinking straw, to push it across the silk in ragged lines. Blow hard directly down onto the paint to create a starry flower-like pattern.

✦ Coat the silk with antifusant and then paint it with layers of very wet paint. Tip the frame and let the colours run down the silk. Turn and tilt it in other directions. Try this with drops of paint to get lines of colour.

✦ Coat the silk with antifusant and then place stencils on the silk. Then spray one or more colours over them. Stencils can be made from: masking tape, cutouts described in 'Chapter 12', leaves, plates, wire or plastic mesh, lace, rice, rock-salt or even smaller grains of salt, uncooked spaghetti, and other objects. Stick the larger stencils onto the silk with double-sided tape if necessary, but do not allow the tape to protrude over the sides, or cover any intentional holes in the stencil. Use a sprayer for a more even flow of paint, or stipple or splatter paint from a toothbrush or other hard-bristled brush. Different effects are achieved if you spray the colours wet on wet or wait for each colour to dry before applying the next. Leave the stencil on until the paint has dried.

✦ A border can be masked off with masking tape before spraying.

✦ Stipple, splatter or spray paint onto silk coated with antifusant, without using a stencil.

✦ Coat the silk with antifusant, then paint it with layers of colour and rock-salt it as in 'Chapter 6'.

✦ Fold or pleat the antifusanted silk (loose, not stretched on a frame) and then spray colour very finely and gently onto the tops of the folds or pleats. Use a different dilution of the same colour, or another colour, to spray into the loosened folds, or move the silk into another folding or pleating before applying the next colour. Folds or pleats can be held in place by clothes pegs: in this case the peg will leave an interesting mark. Alternatively the silk can be knotted or tied in place with string. This last method will give an effect very similar to tie-dyeing.

✦ 'Tartans' can be achieved by making very regular pleats in one direction, spraying, and then pleating in the vertically opposite direction and spraying. Another type of patterning can be obtained by making little 'pyramids' or mounds in the silk by pulling it up at various points, and then spraying.

✦ Scrunch up plastic food wrap and use it to stamp paint onto silk coated with antifusant.

✦ Apply paint to paper cutout shapes with a brush or an eye-dropper. Press the paper, paint-side down, onto silk which has been coated with antifusant, to transfer the paint. Use this method also on silk which has been coated with antifusant and then painted: try it when the paint is still wet, damp or dry, for different results. Details can be painted in after the paint has been applied with the cutout.

✦ Use toothbrushes, hairbrushes, sponges and other objects to stamp the silk coated with antifusant, as described in 'Chapter 12'.

✦ Use sponges, or cut or torn-up pieces of blotting paper, to soak up wet paint from silk which has been coated with antifusant and then painted.

✦ Thicken some of each colour with cornflour, or with carragem, adding a little at a time until the paints are thick but still runny. A bit of practice will help you arrive at the best consistency. Take a spoonful of thickened colour and dribble or splatter it onto the silk in patterns. Tilt the frame to make it travel further if you wish. Do the same with the next colour, until you have covered the silk as much as you want. If you have used cornflour, allow the silk to dry completely and then scrape off the dried cornflour before steaming. After fixing according to 'Chapter 5', wash the silk in warm water to soften the paints.

✦ Add a very dilute solution of antifusant, or plain white spirit to the paints. Do this with very small amounts of paint, because they cannot be separated later. The two will not blend very well but if you shake the jar fairly often a kind of mixing will occur. Paint bold patterns and shapes with this: where the spirit hits the silk there will be a fine white line, or a paler shading of the colour. A more definite effect will be achieved if you coat the silk with antifusant before painting it with this mixture.

DIFFUSANT TECHNIQUE

See colour plate on page 7. Diffusant can be used in conjunction with many other techniques in this book, for example, sugar syrup in 'Chapter 10'. One of the more interesting ways to use it is to turn sharp-edged designs in paint or in fabric pen into soft-blended patterns.

✦ 1. Paint a fine design onto the silk with silk paints, using a very small brush with very little paint on it. Leave areas of white between the colours.

✦ 2. Draw many other lines with fine fabric pens, still leaving white areas in places. Draw these next to the painted designs, not on top of the paint, as pen on top of paint will not diffuse out in step 5.

✦ 3. Let these dry completely.

✦ 4. Mix up a strong solution of diffusant, or lyogen and water: up to 50:50 quantities.

✦ 5. Use an eye-dropper to apply this solution to the painted silk. Drop the diffusant solution all over the silk in little droplets placed close to each other: it helps to touch the eye-dropper to the silk to do this.

✦ 6. Let this dry completely before removing the silk from the frame. As the diffusant dries it will blur and blend the paint and pen lines.

✦ 7. Let the silk rest, and then fix and wash it according to 'Chapter 5'.

✦ 8. Wash the silk in warm soapy water to remove any stiffness from residual diffusant or lyogen.

Variations

✦ Apply the diffusant solution using a paintbrush instead of an eye-dropper. Paint it all over the design, or make a design out of the diffusant solution on top of the paint and fabric pen lines.

✦ Paint the whole of the silk with diffusant solution before painting it with silk paints. Paint while the diffusant is still wet or damp. (This will not work with fabric pens, as they need a dry surface to work.)

✦ Add diffusant directly to the paints, a few drops at a time. This is particularly useful when you want to make the colours run faster and bleed further, for example: when painting a large area or background with a flat smooth colour, without streaking; when rock-salting; when tilting the silk to make stripey blendings of paint, or paint and sugar syrup.

✦ Use a strong diffusant solution instead of water in eye-dropper and other techniques of painting with water explained in 'Chapter 6'.

✦

8
BATIK WITH A DIFFERENCE

Batik is the technique of making designs with hot wax. The word 'batik' is Javanese, meaning to write or draw with wax, and most of us associate this craft with Indonesia.

Like gutta, wax is used as a resist, so that wherever it is applied paint or dye is prevented from entering the fabric. In traditional batik, the fabric is immersed in a dye bath between coats of wax. The techniques explained in this chapter offer a short cut: instead of taking the silk off the frame and dipping it in dyes each time, the colour is simply painted on after each layer of wax.

Having the silk on the frame all the time also allows for greater precision in designing and outlining. The silk is stretched tight, making a stable drawing surface, and the wax does not touch the table or benchtop and therefore is not likely to smear and run through contact with the flat surface.

The one negative aspect of this way of waxing is that to achieve the crackling effect traditionally associated with batik, the silk needs to be taken off the frame so it can be scrunched up to crack the wax. This can be

done before the last coat of paint, however, and thus show at least the one layer of crackling.

Batik involves a certain amount of thinking in reverse, as you must start with your palest colour, and build the design from there. This means that if you have a particular finished product or picture in mind, you will need to carefully think out your design and how to develop it from pale to dark in blocks of line and colour. Once you have laid down the wax there is no way to remove it short of starting all over again with a new piece of silk, so you must be sure to accurately block out areas of shape and colour.

You must also keep in mind how the earlier colours will blend with each successive layer of paint to form secondary and tertiary colours. You can achieve areas of pure colour, but remember that silk paints bleed across the fabric and run into each other if you do not use a resist line of wax or gutta to separate them.

Despite these cautionary statements, batik can be as free-flowing and various as using gutta, and in many ways is easier to do. If you do not want a precise and detailed design, batik is a very simple and exciting technique.

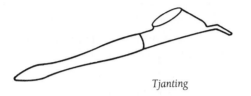

Tjanting

TJANTING (OR CANTING)

The tjanting is a tool used for drawing fine lines in wax. It comes in various shapes and sizes, but generally consists of a small copper cup on a wooden handle. The cup has a fine spout at the bottom through which the wax flows onto the fabric. The cup is dipped into hot wax to fill it, and then the spout is drawn across the fabric as the wax flows out to make a line, or dots.

Using the Tjanting

A tjanting feels strange to use at first because it is not held like a pencil, it has to be used on an angle. The business end (the spout) is angled underneath the handle so that the line does not flow straight from the end as it would from a pencil or brush. With a little practice it becomes fairly easy.

Some hints for successful use are:

◆ Use a mixture of wax that contains more beeswax than usual: 40 - 50 per cent (see below).

◆ The wax must be hot.

◆ Dip the tjanting in the wax frequently to keep the supply in the cup hot and free-flowing.

◆ Keep a tissue or rag in your hand to wipe away drops of wax from the cup and spout each time you dip into the wax and before you bring the tjanting over the silk.

◆ Place your frame of silk on an angle (prop it up on one side).

You will find that you get drops of wax on the silk, and uneven lines at first, so it is essential that you practise using the tjanting on a test frame of silk before you try to use it on a project.

TYPES OF WAX

You can use ordinary candle or paraffin wax in batik, as long as you are using a brush to apply it. When heated it runs out of the tjanting too fast for most people to control, unless very expert. It is also too flakey to achieve a good crackling effect. Pure beeswax is fine in the tjanting, although this level of purity is expensive and not necessary. Beeswax will not crackle because it is too flexible. Most batik is done with varying mixtures of the two: you can mix your own or buy the main types pre-mixed as 'crackling wax' (approximately 30 per cent beeswax and 70 per cent paraffin wax) and 'non-crackling wax' (approximately 40 per cent beeswax and 60 per cent paraffin wax).

HEATING THE WAX

Hot wax is very flammable, so it is wise to use it with care. I have found it easiest, and safest, to use an old electric saucepan or frypan, as this means there is no open flame, and the thermostat keeps the wax at a fairly even temperature close at hand on the workbench. If you are lucky enough to have a pan you can dedicate to this purpose, then you do not have the trouble of cleaning out the wax at the end of each session, but can store it in the electric pan for next time.

If you do not have an electric pan, use an old saucepan on the stove. A double boiler is preferable because it keeps the wax at a more even temperature, and keeps it hot a little longer off the stove.

The wax should be as hot as you would have oil for cooking chips: circulating a bit with the heat, and a fine blue smoke beginning to form. Turn the heat down as soon as the wax begins to smoke. An electric pan with a thermostat light will alert you to fluctuations in temperature. Keep an eye on the wax all the time it is on the stove: do not let it get too hot.

Materials

◆ bucket with lid or large glass jar to hold 2 L (4 pt) of spirit
◆ container in which to heat the wax
◆ design for the project, see 'Chapter 2'
◆ thin disposable gloves or barrier cream for paint
◆ rubber gloves or, better, industrial safety ones for using spirit
◆ paintbrushes: a selection of sizes in hard bristles for applying the wax, and in soft bristles for painting; alternatively, you could use a selection of foambrushes for applying the paint
◆ paints or dyes, tested and diluted according to instructions in 'Chapter 4'
◆ at least 2 pieces of paper the size of the silk: preferably butcher paper or paper towelling, but ordinary newspaper will do
◆ rags, tissues or paper towels
◆ Shellite or white spirit: about 2 L (4 pt)
◆ silk on a frame, prepared according to directions in 'Chapter 2'
◆ scraps of silk, or a test piece stretched on a small frame
◆ tjanting
◆ wax: non-crackling for the tjanting and crackling for the brushwork (see 'Types of Wax')
◆ water

Materials for Variations

◆ cotton buds
◆ cottonwool and peg
◆ gutta applicator pen filled with clear spirit-based gutta, according to directions in 'Chapter 3'
◆ objects to use to print the wax
◆ old newspapers
◆ old blunt knife

BATIK TECHNIQUE

See the lower colour plate on page 6.
◆ 1. Prepare your design, the colours you wish to use, and the silk and frame, by following the steps in 'Chapter 2'.
◆ 2. Use a large paintbrush or foambrush to paint the whole frame of silk the palest colour you are planning to use.
Note: If you want white areas or lines on the design, do not paint the silk before your first waxing.
◆ 3. Allow the colour to dry completely.
◆ 4. While the silk is drying, place the wax in the container and heat it until a faint blue smoke appears, and the wax is gently swirling in the pan. Once it has reached this temperature, turn the heat source down, and keep the wax just below this temperature as best you can. Do not let the wax keep smoking, as the fumes are highly flammable.
◆ 5. Dip your brush into the wax, let it accumulate wax and then wipe off the excess on the side of the container.
◆ 6. Paint the wax onto the areas of your design which you wish to remain the colour you have just painted. Dip your brush in the wax often to be sure that the wax you are applying is hot enough to penetrate right through the silk. You can see that it is going right through when the wax line on the silk is transparent. If the wax is opaque immediately after you have painted it, it was not hot enough and you should dip your brush again and re-wax that area.
◆ 7. Practise using the tjanting on the test piece of silk, by using it to follow steps 8 - 13.

Tilt the frame

◆ 8. Prop up the frame on something which is about 5 cm (2 in) high, at the edge furthest away from you, so that it is tilted at an angle, ready for you to use the tjanting.

✦ 9. Dip the tjanting into the wax, and let it rest there for a few seconds so that the copper cup heats up.

✦ 10. Scoop up a cupful of wax in the bowl of the tjanting.

✦ 11. Working quickly, wipe off the excess wax on the side of the container, and then with a tissue or rag. Make sure no wax is dripping down the side of the cup.

✦ 12. Close the end of the spout with a tissue or rag, and bring the tjanting over the silk.

✦ 13. Remove the tissue or rag, touch the silk gently with the tjanting, and practise drawing lines with the wax which flows out.

✦ 14. When you are satisfied with the degree of control you have over the flow of wax from the tjanting, you can then follow steps 8 - 13 on your proper batik silk piece. Use the tjanting to make finer lines where you want your project silk to stay the first colour.

✦ 15. When you have finished using the tjanting, lay the frame flat again and allow the wax to set: about 5 to 10 minutes. Do not use a hair dryer to try and speed this process, as it will only serve to melt the wax. Similarly do not put the frame out in the sun on a hot summer day: this may well be enough to melt the wax and blur your lines.

✦ 16. Dip a large paintbrush or foambrush into the jar of your second-palest colour, wipe excess paint off on the side of the jar and paint over the whole frame of silk, wax included.

✦ 17. If you do not want speckles of this colour to remain in the areas where you have waxed, wipe them off the wax with a rag. A scrap of silk is good to do this: you will end up with some pretty silk pieces just from wiping up excess paint.

✦ 18. Let this coat of paint dry completely before going on to the next step.

✦ 19. Repeat steps 5 - 6, and then steps 8 - 13, to block out areas of the second colour.

✦ 20. Repeat steps 15 - 18 to apply the second coat of colour.

✦ 21. Repeat the process until you have all the layers of wax and paint that you want.

✦ 22. Allow the paint to dry completely before attempting to remove the wax. It is best to leave the silk on the frame while it is drying.

✦ 23. Remove the silk from the frame.

✦ 24. Place it between two layers of paper, each layer as large as the piece of silk.

✦ 25. Iron with a hot iron to melt the wax out.

✦ 26. If a lot of wax remains in the silk after the first ironing, repeat the process using new paper.

✦ 27. Rinse out the rest of the wax in white spirit or Shellite. Remember that these are highly flammable substances, so keep them away from naked flames, and protect your hands with industrial safety gloves or rubber gloves. Place the silk in a bucket or large jar of Shellite or white spirit, and squeeze it as if you were washing it, until it is completely soaked in the spirit.

✦ 28. Let the silk sit in the spirit for at least 10 minutes, or longer.

✦ 29. Squeeze out excess spirit back into the bucket.

✦ 30. Hang the silk out to dry, making sure no water gets near it. Drying should only take a few minutes, unless there is still a lot of wax in the silk.

✦ 31. If there is still wax in the silk, for example if it feels slightly greasy, or even slimy, then repeat steps 27 - 30. You may need to dispose of the first lot of spirit you used, and use clean spirit, if there is too much wax in the original bucket.

Note: If you are going to be doing a lot of batik it is useful to keep the waxy spirit in a sealed container, and use it for the first rinse each time. It will need to be disposed of carefully once it is so waxy that it adds more wax than it takes out. You can also take the wax out directly with spirit without having to iron it first, but this very quickly pollutes the spirit beyond a usable level.

◆ 32. Let the silk rest, and then fix and wash it according to the instructions in 'Chapter 5'.

Variations

One set of variations is to use different implements and methods to apply the wax:
◆ Use a cotton bud.
◆ Use a cottonwool ball held in a peg (this can also be used to apply the paint).
◆ Try various objects to print the wax onto the silk by a stamping method. The most sophisticated way is to obtain a 'tjap', a Javanese printing block made with copper strips soldered together to form a design. Failing this, try out the various methods of stencilling and printing outlined in 'Chapter 12', but note that screen printing will not work because the wax will clog the screen.
◆ Apply the wax by splattering, or by various brush strokes including lines and dots, and by dry-brush techniques (made with a very stiff brush with little wax on it, so that the lines of wax are separated where the bristles of the brush are separated as you press down hard).

Another set of variations involves using clear spirit-based gutta:
◆ Apply clear spirit-based gutta instead of wax in a tjanting in steps 8 - 15 above, to draw the fine lines of the design. This is generally easier to do than using wax. However, the paint should not be applied straight over the top of the gutta lines as it can be over lines of wax: some of the paint will sink into the gutta and discolour the painted silk underneath. Thus, you need to paint around or next to the gutta lines, not over them.
◆ Combine a gutta design, painted as normal, with a crackling effect achieved by waxing all over the painted silk with crackling wax. Remove the silk from the frame once the wax has set, and scrunch it up to make cracks. Then immerse the silk in paint, or lay it on newspaper and paint the whole piece, or attach it to the frame again and paint it. The

result will be a delicate gutta design with a batik crackling effect superimposed.
Note: This will not work with the spirit-based coloured guttas, because when you take the wax out with spirit, the coloured gutta will smear, or come out completely.
◆ Wax can also be used to 'save' mistakes: this is done by waxing over the bits you like of things which have gone wrong, and then painting over the rest to cover up the bits you do not like. This is not completely foolproof because any gutta lines will remain and original colours can show through.

Another set of variations is based on combinations of the various painting techniques and wax:
◆ Paint the silk all over with many colours, and let it dry. Then wax a design, using only one layer of wax. Paint all over the silk again, with either one or several darker colours.
◆ Paint many colours carefully onto the silk so that they do not run into each other and so that they form a design. Let them dry. Wax over the parts where each colour remains clear, then paint over the whole fabric with a dark colour. Black gives a very striking effect at this stage, covering up any areas of colour not protected by wax. See the upper colour plate on page 6.
◆ Paint the silk in various colours or one colour, then use the tjanting or a clear gutta pen to outline a design, and paint within those lines as if it were white silk. When the wax is removed the lines will be coloured by the first layer of paint.

The final set of variations is to wax over the whole piece of silk:
◆ Let the wax set and then use a dull knife to etch a pattern into the wax, then paint the silk all over. The paint will only penetrate the fabric where there are etched lines in the wax. The all-over waxing can be done before the silk is painted at all, or at any stage during the batik process, but once it has been done no

more layers can be added.

♦ Let the wax set and then 'crackle' it by scrunching up the silk. Then paint over it to let the paint run into the cracks. This is best done at the last layer of wax if you are following the short-cut batik method described in the step-by-step guide above. You need to either loosen the silk on the frame or, even better, remove it from the frame altogether, so that you can scrunch it up to get the crackling effect.

CLEANING WAXY INSTRUMENTS

The wax is best removed from the paintbrushes by soaking them in white spirit or Shellite. The container used to heat the wax can be cleaned in the same way, but if it is to be used for cooking after that, *which I would not recommend*, you must let it dry out completely after cleaning with spirit, and then wash it thoroughly in hot soapy water.

♦

9

Mop–Ups

'Mop-ups' are the result of a technique which I discovered by using scraps of silk to mop up paints I had spilled, or to mop up the excess when I had put too much paint onto a large piece of silk.

Some of the rags turned out to be beautiful opalescent blendings of colour, full of fire and light. Of course some of them turned out to be just ugly rags! The trick is to start with a good variety of colours on the large piece of silk (the 'base piece'), to use several pieces of silk for mopping up the paint (the 'mop-up pieces'), and to stop mopping up at just the right time. You need to mop up just enough to keep the colours separate without being blotchy, but not so much that the silk is saturated and the colour all blends into grey or brown.

Lovely mop-ups can be made with most weaves and weights of silk, and I like to do several different types of silk in each mop-up session. The results are different on each type of silk, but jacquards are especially beautiful because the patterning in the silk adds another dimension to the blending of the colours.

The heavier the weight of silk, the harder it is to achieve a good blending without the colours remaining too streaky or blotchy. The danger is then that one tends to keep going too long, adding more paint in an attempt to blend out the blobs, and the end result is an overly blended, bland wash of one muddy colour.

Finished pieces also differ according to the range of colours used in the base piece, and the point at which you decide to stop adding more colour and let the mop-up piece dry.

This method is suitable for very large pieces as well as smaller ones. I usually use a 3 m by 115 cm (3¼ yd by 45 in) piece as the base, and have mop-up pieces as long as 5 m (5½ yd) from it. However, you can start with a much smaller piece if you wish. Suit the size of your base piece to the size of the largest piece you want in the end: the base piece may be smaller, but not by a big margin. For example, it is relatively easy to mop-up a 3.5 m (4 yd) piece from a 3 m (3¼ yd) base, but much harder to do a 5 m (5½ yd) piece from a base of that size.

It is a good idea to do several pieces in one session, as this is a quick technique using a lot of wet paint.

Materials
+ gloves, thin disposable type, or barrier cream
+ large paintbrushes, preferably one for each colour
+ paints or dyes diluted and tested according to directions in 'Chapter 4', but note step 4 below
+ rags, tissues or paper towels
+ scissors
+ silk: one piece on a frame according to

instructions in 'Chapter 2', but note step 1 below

✦ other loose pieces, prepared as described in 'Chapter 2'

✦ water

Materials for Variations

✦ eye-dropper

✦ rock-salt

✦ wax, and batik implements

✦ pens filled with gutta as described in 'Chapter 3'

✦ pegs

MOP-UP TECHNIQUE

✦ 1. Attach a piece of silk to the frame following steps 1 - 6, 'Attaching the Silk to the Frame' (page 28). This will be the base for painting several other pieces, so suit its size to the largest piece you wish to have at the end. Attach it very tightly, with the staples or pins closer together than usual, so that it does not sag with wet paint.

✦ 2. Cut as many other pieces of silk as you wish to complete in the session. These can be up to 50 per cent longer than the base piece, or any size smaller than it.

✦ 3. Keep these pieces close by, ready to use, because once you start you will need to work fairly quickly.

✦ 4. Following steps 1 - 9, 'Colour Mixing and Testing' (page 37), mix up to 250 mL ($^1/_2$ pt) quantities of each of the colours you wish to use, fairly dilute (for example, 50:50 paint and water) as this method uses quite a lot of paint and involves layering of the colours, so that diluting with too little water is wasteful. Stronger dilutions may be fine if you wish to have very dark or intense results, but you will find that it is not really necessary. The quantity of each diluted colour will depend on how many pieces of silk you intend to mop-up in the session, and how heavy the weights of the silks are.

Note: Try using all the colours of the rainbow as your base paints. These are red, orange, yellow, bright green, light blue, dark blue, purple ... and hot pink for good measure.

✦ 5. Set the jars of paint out in the order you wish to use them, with the lids off, so you can work very quickly. Colours which are close to each other on the spectrum will blend into each other easily on the silk.

✦ 6. Using a large paintbrush with lots of paint on it, paint wide stripes of each colour from one side of the silk to the other.

✦ 7. If you are only using one paintbrush, wash it between colours so as not to contaminate the next jar of paint. Squeeze out excess water before putting the brush into the next colour, so that you do not dilute the paint each time.

✦ 8. Quickly blend each successive colour into the one which went before, but do not spend long on this as speed is more important. The aim is to have all the colours still very wet at the end.

✦ 9. If you take longer the first time and the first one or two colours are almost dry when you have finished laying down all the colours, go back and quickly add more paint to those stripes before going on to the next step.

✦ 10. Take one of the prepared cut pieces of silk, and lay it down on top of the wet painted silk.

✦ 11. Pat it down gently (with gloved hands!) and let it soak up some of the paint. It does not need to soak up paint all over: patches of white are acceptable at this stage.

✦ 12. Pick it up and turn it around so that different colours are now underneath the ones already soaked.

✦ 13. Lie it down on the wet painted silk again, pat it down and let it soak up some more of the paint.

✦ 14. Repeat steps 12 and 13 until this mop-up piece of silk is covered in paint.

✦ 15. If unwanted white patches remain, and you have soaked up all the excess paint from the base piece, use a big paintbrush to paint colour directly onto those patches.

✦ 16. Do not repeat steps 12 and 13 so often that your mop-up piece is dripping with paint, as the silk will not be able to accommodate that much paint, and all the colours will over-blend and become muddy. It may take a few tries before you know just when to stop.

✦ 17. Take the mop-up piece and scrunch it or gently wring it so that all the colours blend a little or a lot, depending on the final effect you want.

✦ 18. If the silk is too dry for much blending to occur, sprinkle water on it and then scrunch or wring it. You can also sprinkle dilute paint onto it instead of water if you feel that your mop-up is in danger of becoming too pale in this process, but be careful: sprinkling paint on it at this stage can result in blotches.

✦ 19. If you want the colours to blend more, then leave the mop-up piece twisted or scrunched up for a while before you hang it out. Keep checking on it to see that it has not 'gone too far', and that stripes of colour are not being formed in the twists and folds of fabric (unless you want them to be).

✦ 20. Hang the mop-up piece of silk on the line to dry. Some further blending will occur as it is drying on the line, so if you want the colours to stay as they are without much more blending occurring, throw the fabric in the clothes drier for a few minutes on warm, before you hang it out.

✦ 21. While that piece is drying, paint the base piece again with the rainbow colours, or whatever combination you have chosen, and repeat the whole process with the next piece of prepared cut silk.

✦ 22. Repeat the whole process for each piece of silk.

✦ 23. Let the silk rest, and then fix and wash it according to the instructions in 'Chapter 5'.

Variations

The main ways to vary a mop-up are:
✦ Use different sets of colours in the base paints.
✦ Use different weights and weaves of silk.
✦ Stop mopping up at different stages of blending.
✦ Add water or paint to the silk before you scrunch it and wring it at step 18.
✦ Dry it quickly, or slowly, to allow more or less blending. See colour plate on page 9.

Other variations which will give you results quite different from the usual mop-up include:
✦ At steps 18, 19 and 20, leave the silk fairly wet with paint, twist it very tightly, and peg it on the line so that it remains twisted while it dries. The paint will accumulate in the folds of silk and you will end up with a piece that has darker stripes of colour in an uneven pattern. You can then iron out the folds before you steam the silk for a smooth, flat silk piece. If you leave the creases in during steaming, your silk will have permanent crease marks, which can also be very pretty.
✦ Let the mop-up dry completely, then attach it to the frame and use it as a background piece to paint on as normal. The piece on the cover of this book, 'Lasseter's Reef' was painted in this way. Remember that the background mop-up colours will influence and change any colours you put over the top.
✦ Use the mop-up as a background or base for any of the other techniques in this book.

USING THE BASE PIECE

The base piece of silk will also be very pretty in the end, covered with many layers of colour. You can leave it as it is, or sprinkle rock-salt on it, as long as the colours are still wet after the last mop-up. If not, paint them again first.

Variations

✦ When you have finished the mop-ups, apply water to the base piece of silk with an eye-dropper, or by sprinkling or spraying, to mottle the colour.

✦ When you have finished the mop-ups, paint stripes of very wet paint on the base piece going the opposite way to the original stripes. Leave it at that, or tilt the frame and let lines of paint flow down, then tilt it another way for new directions of flow, and so on.

✦ Leave the last mop-up on top of the base piece on the frame so that it has wrinkles, and bubbles of air form between the two pieces of silk. Let the two pieces dry together. Lighter and darker lines and shapes will form according to where the two are touching or not touching.

✦ Let the base piece dry, then wax a design on it and paint over the top.

✦ Perform any other of the techniques covered in this book, using the base piece as a background.

✦

10

SUGAR SYRUP

The use of sugar syrup in fabric painting has only relatively recently been introduced from France. At first it was used like gutta in serti (see 'Introduction'), but several different ways of using it have now evolved. The main methods are explained in this chapter.

Basically, a syrup of sugar and water is cooked up and then painted onto silk which either has been painted with a pale background or left white. Paint is then applied next to the sugar, or onto it, or both. The sugar acts like an antifusant in that it prevents the paint from bleeding evenly. Where the paint meets the sugar syrup, it eats away at it and so enters the fabric in unpredictable ways.

Differing effects can be achieved depending on how hot and how thick the syrup is, how it is applied (over the whole silk, in lines, splattered, and so on), where the paint is placed (next to it, or on it), and how many layers of sugar and paint are applied. The end results are interesting, but not always beautiful. They can be reminiscent of tie-dyeing.

Materials
+ caster sugar, 1 cup
+ water, 1 cup
Note: This will make enough sugar syrup for 1 or 2 large pieces of silk, say 115 cm (45 in) square
+ thin disposable gloves or barrier cream
+ paintbrushes: 1 or 2 large sizes each of hard-bristled ones for the syrup, and soft-bristled ones or foambrushes for the paint

+ paints or dyes diluted and tested as in 'Chapter 4'
Note: The paint will dry paler from sugar syrup than in normal techniques
+ newspaper to protect the work area from syrup splattering
+ rags, tissues or paper towels
+ saucepan and heat source (stove)
+ silk on a frame, prepared according to instructions in 'Chapter 2'
+ wooden spoon
+ water

Materials for Variations
+ antifusant
+ diffusant
+ cottonwool balls
+ eye-dropper
+ paint sprayer
+ sponges, brushes and other objects for printing
+ teaspoon

MAKING THE SUGAR SYRUP
+ 1. Dissolve the sugar and water in the saucepan.
+ 2. Heat the mixture to boiling point, stirring continuously.
+ 3. Turn the heat down so that the mixture is simmering.
+ 4. Continue to stir the syrup and keep watching to make sure it does not go brown, or stick to the bottom of the saucepan.
+ 5. The syrup will slowly thicken as it cooks.

It can be used at any stage after it has begun to thicken: the effects obtained will be different according to how thick the syrup has become. *Note:* The syrup can be used hot or cold, but the hotter the syrup the more striking the effect. Unused syrup can be stored in a glass jar with a lid, and will keep for a long time. If it becomes crystallised, dissolve it with a little boiling water, pour it back into a saucepan, and reheat it to the desired thickness.

BASIC STRIPING TECHNIQUE

✦ 1. Paint the whole of the silk with a pale background colour. This can be a single flat colour, or a grading of dilutions of one colour, or several colours.
✦ 2. Let this dry.
✦ 3. Use a hard-bristled brush to paint lines of sugar syrup along the fabric.
✦ 4. Leave some space between the lines, although it does not matter if the syrup runs together in places.
✦ 5. Paint quickly and in long repetitive strokes. The lines do not need to be even: let them come out thinner or thicker as the brush happens to hit the silk. Blobs of syrup on the silk are fine, too: they will form interesting areas of colour.
✦ 6. As soon as you have finished with the syrup, use a soft-bristled brush to apply lots of paint in the spaces between the lines. Do not wait for the syrup to dry, as the effect will work better if the paint is added straight away.
✦ 7. Paint quickly and without worrying about the paint going on to the syrup lines: it should do so to a certain extent, to start off the process of eating away the syrup.
✦ 8. Use as many different colours as you like.
✦ 9. Leave the painting to dry. This can take a long time, even several days, depending on the heat and humidity. The paint and the syrup will continue to work together as long as the piece remains wet, so you can see your painting slowly change.

Note: You can hurry along this process by using a hair dryer, but you must be extremely careful not to use it on too hot a setting, nor to let the dryer get too close to the silk. And move it constantly, as you can turn the syrup to toffee.
✦ 10. Make sure the painting is as close to dry as possible before you remove it from the frame and fix it by one of the methods in 'Chapter 5'. Silk which has had sugar syrup painted on it must be rolled in double paper for steaming, as a lot of the colour comes out onto the paper, and so there is a danger that it will transfer through onto the next piece of silk.
✦ 11. After fixing, rinse the silk in cold water until no more colour comes out. Then wash the silk in mild soap and tepid water to remove any remaining sugar syrup. Do not soak it at this stage, as the warmth of the water may make the colours run.

Variations

✦ Instead of painting a pale background, spray several colours onto the silk, then paint your syrup, and then spray more colours over the top.
✦ Paint widely separated stripes of sugar syrup directly onto white silk. Fill the gaps between the stripes with colour, paint more syrup stripes onto the paint, and then paint another layer of colour.

CHEQUERED TECHNIQUE

✦ 1. Hold or lean your frame of silk so that it is on a sharp incline.
Note: Work as quickly as you can through the next steps, applying the syrup as rapidly as possible so that it is still wet when you come to do the painting.
✦ 2. Use a teaspoon, or an eye-dropper if your syrup is not too hot, to apply large drops of sugar syrup to the top edge of the silk, enough so that a line of it runs down the silk to the other side of the frame.

✦ 3. If your syrup line does not quite reach the other side, add a bit more syrup either at the top starting point, in which case you will have a thicker line at the top, or halfway down, in which case you will have thicker lines in the middle. It is not easy to get lines of equal thickness all the way across the silk, and really that is not what you should be aiming for: the fun of this method is in the unpredictable result.

✦ 4. Start the next line of syrup about 2 cm (1 in) further along the edge, and so on, until you have lines of syrup going all the way across the silk from one side to the other.

✦ 5. Turn the frame around so that the adjacent side is now on top, and dribble lines of syrup down this side, as you did before, so that these new lines form a chequered pattern when they cross the first set of lines. Continue making lines all the way along this side, as you did on the previous side.

✦ 6. As soon as you have finished putting on the syrup, use an eye-dropper to apply several different colours of paint, in the same way as you did the sugar. Let the paint run down the spaces in between the lines of syrup.

✦ 7. Apply paint first to one side, then turn the frame around and apply it to the other, so that the lines cross, as did the sugar syrup lines.

✦ 8. Lay the frame flat and let the silk dry. This might take several days if the weather is humid, or cool.

✦ 9. When the silk is as close to dry as possible, remove it from the frame and fix and wash as for the striping technique. Remember to use double paper if you are using a steamer.

Variations

✦ Make your stripes of syrup, and of paint, go diagonally from corner to corner. This is a little harder to do in that it is harder to hold and balance the frame as you work.

✦ Apply stripes of syrup and paint in one direction only. This could also be done diagonally across the silk.

✦ Before you start, cover your whole frame of silk with a mixture of a few drops of diffusant in a little water. While this is still damp, apply lines of sugar syrup either in one direction, or crossing, or diagonally, as above. Apply the paints in the same way, as quickly as you can. The end result will be softer, more fluid lines of colour.

SPLATTERING TECHNIQUE

See colour plate on page 14.

This method is very messy, so do it outside, or cover all your workspace, within about 1 m (3 ½ ft) of your frame of silk, with old newspapers.

✦ 1. Dip a large brush into the sugar syrup. Allow it to soak up a lot of syrup.

✦ 2. Splatter the syrup all over the silk. Use hard sharp motions so that you splatter drops rather than stripes of syrup.

✦ 3. While the syrup is still wet, use an eye-dropper to apply drops of paint all over the silk, on the syrup and next to it. Use several different colours.

✦ 4. Splatter more sugar syrup over the top of the painted silk.

✦ 5. Leave the silk to dry as much as possible before removing it from the frame. This technique can take even longer to dry than the others, because of the heavy layers of sugar.

✦ 6. Fix and wash as for the striping technique. Remember: use double paper in the steamer!

Variations

✦ Paint the silk before splattering.

✦ Coat the silk with diffusant and water before splattering.

PRINTING WITH SUGAR SYRUP

You can use all sorts of objects found in the home to print the sugar syrup onto the silk: sponges, scrubbing pads, kitchen and nail brushes, mesh and so on. A large paintbrush with stiff bristles can also be used. I have used a large-holed sponge in the following guide, but you can substitute many different objects to obtain a variety of effects.

✦ 1. Place the sponge gently onto the surface of the sugar syrup solution, so that it takes up some of the syrup, but does not become soaked and drip.

✦ 2. Gently touch the silk with the sponge and press it down slightly, so that the syrup is transferred without spreading out past the sponge.

✦ 3. Dip and print until you have a pattern all over your silk.

✦ 4. Spray the paint on while the syrup is still wet. Use several colours, and spray them in layers, or next to each other.

✦ 5. Allow the silk to dry as much as possible, over a few days, before removing it from the frame.

✦ 6. Fix and wash as for the striping technique. Do not forget: use double paper in the steamer.

GENERAL VARIATIONS

✦ Spray the paint onto the silk after applying sugar syrup, rather than painting or dropping it on.

✦ Apply a coat of antifusant, and let this dry before you start. You can cover the whole frame of silk with antifusant, or just cover parts of it. You can do this to white silk, or to silk which has been painted a background colour or colours. The simplest way of applying the antifusant is to dip a cottonwool ball into your container of antifusant, and use this ball to rub the antifusant evenly over the silk. Use this silk as a base for any of the techniques of applying sugar syrup, except the variations with diffusant, of course. Generally speaking, the best effects after using antifusant are obtained if you spray the paint on rather than dropping or brushing it on.

✦

11

MARBLING

Marbling is an old technique, used principally in the Western world for creating rippling effects on endpapers in bookbinding. It was a neglected art for most of this century but has been revived in the last decade or so. Paint is not applied directly, but is picked up onto the material from colours floated in patterns on the surface of a bath of sizing, usually liquid seaweed. It is more often done on paper, but recent research has rediscovered methods for use on fabric.

Marbling can be a messy process, and it is not easy to get a perfect finish. Unlike painting, the details of the patterning cannot be completely controlled. However, as in the sugar syrup method, the unpredictable nature of the results is part of the fun of this technique. It is also extremely quick to do, once you have set up your materials.

Marbling should be done near a water source, preferably a hose outside or a tap and a large sink, to rinse off the sizing. Since humidity and air temperature can have significant effects on the inks and the sizing bath, you will need to weigh up the benefits of doing it outside, where the mess does not matter, and inside, where you can keep the environment cool and humid. Avoid marbling in the hottest parts of the day, and avoid working in direct sunlight.

Marbling Kits

Japanese marbling kits are now available from many craft stores. These consist mainly of inks,
and small circles of paper to drop them onto in a bath of water, so that the colours spread rather than sink. These kits are quite good fun, but take a bit of practice at first. It is not easy to get the paints to stay on the surface. They are limited, however, in the range of effects and depth of colour that can be achieved.

Materials

+ alum, 30 g (1 oz), available from chemists
+ antiseptic, 1 teaspoon, or 2 Campden tablets, available from craft suppliers
+ blender
+ brushes, sticks or eye-droppers to drop paints, one for each colour
+ carragem powder, 1 tablespoon per 1.3 L (2⁴/₅ pt) of water, available from craft suppliers
+ fabric marbling inks (see 'Colours' below)
+ flat pan, larger than the material to be marbled
+ gloves, thin disposable type, or barrier cream
+ marbling combs, or sticks, forks, haircombs, toothbrushes (see 'Marbling Combs' below, to make your own)
+ old newspapers
+ ox gall, 2 - 3 drops per tablespoonful of colour (optional), available from craft suppliers
+ overflow box or tray (optional)
+ silk, washed according to the instructions in 'Chapter 2' – pieces to marble, and scraps for testing
+ spoons: tablespoons and teaspoons
+ water: preferably rainwater or distilled water, enough to make a carragem bath to a depth of 5 cm (2 in) in the flat pan

✦ tapwater for rinsing the dropping implements, also 600 mL (1⅓ pt) for diluting the alum

✦ white spirit to dilute the marbling inks, if you are using marbling inks which are diluted with this substance (see 'Colours' below)

Materials for Variations
✦ albumen (eggwhite)
✦ fine sticks
✦ masking tape
✦ needles
✦ olive oil
✦ turpentine oil
✦ washing-up detergent
✦ wax

COLOURS

Marbling inks are different from the silk paints used in other projects in this book. They need to have a very finely ground pigment which will not sink to the bottom of the sizing bath, and to be readily dispersed when floated on the surface. In addition, they must be able to be rinsed in water to remove the sizing before they are fixed: this is impossible for the silk paints we have been dealing with so far.

Fabric marbling inks can be bought ready-made: these are diluted with white spirit. You can try screen-printing inks, water-based acrylics and some calligraphy inks, but the results can be very variable. Ox gall can be added to help dispersion, although this is not always necessary, especially with ready-bought fabric marbling inks.

Whatever colours you decide to use, dilute them to the consistency of cream and then test them on the surface of the marbling bath, to see if you have the right composition and dilution for them to float and to spread out to about 5 cm (2 in) in diameter.

When mixing the colours to get particular hues and intensities, remember that they will end up paler after marbling than they would if painted directly on the fabric.

SIZING BATH

You can use substances such as wallpaper glue or a cornflour and water mix to make the bath, but more consistent results are achieved using carragem.

The bath should be prepared at least the night before a marbling session. It can be used again and again during the session. If enough is left over it can be stored and used days and weeks later, provided you have mixed in some preservative (Campden tablets) or antiseptic to kill algae.

Making a Carragem Bath

You need 1 tablespoon of carragem powder per 1.3 L (2⅘ pt) of water (preferably rainwater or distilled water) to make the bath: the total volume of course depends on the size of the pan you wish to fill.

✦ 1. Mix 1 tablespoon of powder with enough cold water to make a paste.

✦ 2. Place this in a blender.

✦ 3. Slowly add the lukewarm water, blending all the time.

✦ 4. When you have reached 1.3 L (2⅘ pt), blend the mixture for a few more minutes, to break down as many opaque lumps as you can. The resulting mixture should be clear, pale honey-coloured, and gelatinous but liquid.

✦ 5. Pour the mixture into the pan you will be using for marbling.

✦ 6. Repeat steps 1 - 5 until you have filled the pan to a depth of at least 5 cm (2 in).

✦ 7. Add two dissolved Campden tablets, or a teaspoon of antiseptic, and mix this in thoroughly.

✦ 8. Leave the mixture overnight for the bath to mature.

PREPARING THE SILK

Most materials require mordanting with alum before the marbling inks will adhere to them. While some would argue that this is not necessary for silk, I have found that more often than not the colours will just flake off if this is not done first. I usually prepare several pieces of silk, and also lots of paper, at a time. This way, I have enough articles to make the session worthwhile, and also have scraps on which to test colour dilutions.

✦ 1. Mix 30 g (1 oz) of alum with 600 mL (1⅓ pt) of hot water.

✦ 2. Stir the solution until the alum has dissolved.

✦ 3. Leave it to cool.

✦ 4. Dip the fabric into the solution, making sure it is fully immersed.

✦ 5. Hang the silk out to dry. Let it dry naturally: if heated unevenly it will work unevenly in the marbling.

MARBLING COMBS

Combs are used to make the patterns associated with traditional marbling. Marbling can be done without combing at all, or by using substitutes such as sticks, forks, haircombs, toothbrushes, and other objects found in the house. Simple marbling combs can be bought ready-made, or you can make them yourself. Others needed for distinctive pattern types cannot be bought: detailed instructions for making these are given in Grunebaum's *How to Marbleize Paper* (see the 'Supplementary Reading List').

Making a Simple Marbling Comb

✦ 1. Make two strips of thick cardboard or fine plywood 5 cm (2 in) wide and long enough to fit conveniently into the marbling tray.

✦ 2. Measure a line along one strip so that the whole strip is divided in two horizontally.

✦ 3. Score a shallow line along this with a Stanley knife.

✦ 4. Measure spaces about 1 cm (½ in) apart along this line.

✦ 5. At every measured point, draw a line down to the bottom of the strip, and score it as you did the horizontal line.

✦ 6. Glue long pins or needles into each of

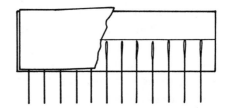

Making a marbling comb

these lines, so that they protrude 2 cm (1 in) from the bottom. Make sure they protrude an equal distance so that they are all forming a straight line at the tips.

✦ 7. Glue the second strip over the first, to seal in the pins or needles.

✦ 8. Leave this to dry, and then varnish the cardboard or wood.

MARBLING TECHNIQUE

✦ 1. Prepare the workspace with protective newspaper. Cover the benchtop, and place paper on other surfaces where you can lay the marbled silk on it to dry.

✦ 2. Make a pile of sheets or strips of newspaper to skim the carragem bath after each application of colour.

✦ 3. Fill the marbling tray with the carragem bath prepared previously.

✦ 5. Skim the surface of the carragem to remove any dust particles or film which may have developed overnight. Do this by laying a sheet of newspaper on the surface, gently patting it down, and then lifting it off again; or, skim a strip of newspaper along the surface to one end of the bath where the film or dust can be scooped up over the side into an overflow box or tray, or onto the newspaper-covered workbench.

✦ 6. Dilute the colours to the consistency of cream, using a few drops of ox gall in each, if desired. Mix colours together for different hues, or leave them pure. It is a good idea to start with only two or three colours at first, until you get used to controlling them on the carragem bath.

✦ 7. Test each colour by sprinkling a few drops from a brush, eye-dropper, spoon or stick onto the surface of the bath. Dip the implement into the paint, then hold it closely over the carragem and gently shake or tap it to release the paint. Do not flick the paint off: it will splatter everywhere.

✦ 8. Each drop should spread rapidly to a circle of about 5 cm (2 in) in diameter. If the colour does not spread far enough, or a lot of it sinks to the bottom, dilute it further or add more ox gall. If it spreads too far, thicken it with more pure colour. If the colour breaks up, it needs to be mixed more thoroughly. If the colour continues to sink to the bottom no matter how much you dilute it, the problem could be with the carragem bath. It may be too thick, or too cold, or have too many impurities in it.

✦ 9. Skim the bath between colours, to clean the surface.

✦ 10. When you have all the colours you wish to use diluted to the right consistency, sprinkle them one by one onto the surface of the carragem.

Note: The colour first sprinkled on the bath tends to spread the furthest, and there are some colours which spread further than others. Therefore it is important to work quickly to get all the colours down, and to do this in the order which will give you the result you want. Generally speaking, metallic gold, white and colours mixed with white should go down first, pure colours next, and yellow and metallic silver last.

✦ 11. Do not sprinkle too much colour on: it is best to have just enough for each drop to be able to spread out and not remain too concentrated on one spot.

✦ 12. You can leave the colours in the pattern formed through dropping them on the surface, as in the colour plate on page 15, or you can comb them, or use any of the methods listed in 'Variations' below to create patterns – before picking up the paint onto the silk. Do not play around with the patterning too much or you will cause the paint to break up.

✦ 13. The first time you do marbling, or use particular dilutions of colour, follow steps 14 - 20 using scraps of silk to test out dilutions and to test whether the alum has worked properly.

✦ 14. Lift your prepared silk by diagonally opposite corners. If you have someone to help you, it is good to hold all four corners, especially with large pieces.

✦ 15. Without folding or creasing, lay the silk down onto the patterned colours. Do not drag it across the surface as this can smear the colours. Let it touch down at the middle first, and gradually lower the corners from there. Do this gently and slowly, trying to maintain an even movement. Do not push the fabric below the surface, which would marble on the other side of the fabric. Do not cause ripples in the bath, which would make the colours run into wave patterns. Do not trap air bubbles, which would leave the silk white.

✦ 16. Let go of the silk, and then gently pat it down so that any air bubbles are pushed out.

✦ 17. When you can see the design through the back of the silk, with no white patches showing, this means that the surface of the silk is all in contact with the paints, and the marbling is complete. Take two corners from one end and gently lift the silk up from the carragem, taking care not to drag it across and smear the paint.

✦ 18. Rinse the silk quickly and thoroughly under running water to remove excess carragem. Let the water run over it – do not rub or scrunch it.

✦ 19. Lay the silk out flat, on spread newspaper, and let it dry. If this is in a windy spot, weight the corners down carefully: if the silk folds over on itself the colours can smear.

✦ 20. Skim the surface of the carragem bath to remove any paint particles.

✦ 21. Repeat steps 10 - 20 for each piece of silk you wish to marble.

✦ 22. When all the silks are completely dry

(which can take 1 – 2 days with some inks) set the colour in the fabric by the method recommended for those inks. This is usually accomplished by ironing it between two sheets of paper towelling.

Variations

✦ You can mask out areas of the silk, or a border around the edge, using masking tape.
✦ Wax can be used to draw a design on the silk before any marbling is done, but you will need to use fabric paints which can be immersed in white spirit, or remove the wax by ironing and then washing in hot water.
✦ Another way of causing white areas, this time unevenly, is to drop a mixture of washing-up detergent and water on some areas instead of paint (a few drops of detergent in half a cup of water).
✦ Take a second pick-up, on a new sheet of silk, from the same patterned colours, before you skim them from the surface of the bath. This second 'print' will be paler than the first so you need to be careful that there are no blank areas.
✦ Do two pick-ups on the one piece of silk, to get two layers of patterned colour. It is better if the first one is to dry before you do the second.
✦ Drop new colour onto colours which you have just combed into a pattern; this will push aside the first layer.
✦ Add alum to the colour to make it break up into flower-like shapes on the surface. This will not work with all types of inks, so experiment.
✦ Add some albumen (eggwhite) to the colour: this should make it form starry patterns on the surface. Again, this may not work with all inks.
✦ Add a few drops of olive oil to the paints, and then sprinkle the colours onto the surface in a vigorous way so that many drops are formed quickly and so that they do not spread

too far. The oil will narrow the white veins which form between the colours. After fixing the colour in the silk, wash it in hot soapy water to remove the oil.
✦ Modify the last variation by dropping turpentine oil onto the coloured and patterned marble bath before picking the colours up onto the silk.

Variations of Combing

✦ Draw a stick through the colours in random patterns.
✦ Use fine sticks, or needles, to draw shapes in repeated patterns in the colours. The thicker the carragem bath the more control you have at this stage of drawing, but you still need to draw very slowly and carefully so that the colours do not break up. Push and pull the colours, holding a stick or needle in each hand, to get the desired shapes.
✦ Draw straight parallel lines in the paint with a stick.
✦ Draw a simple comb across the paint, so that parallel lines result.
✦ Do both of the above, using the comb in lines vertically opposite to the lines made by the stick.
✦ Draw the simple comb through the paint in zigzag patterns.
✦ Draw a stick through the paint in spirals, to make snail patterns.
✦ Do the same with a comb, or comb the colours and then turn that pattern into spirals with a stick.
✦ Create a wave pattern by gently moving the sizing tray back and forth, or by moving the paper across the surface of the bath in a similar way.
✦ For other more difficult patterns, such as the bouquet and peacock patterns, consult Grunebaum's book (see the 'Supplementary Reading List').

✦

12
PRINTING, STENCILLING AND STAMPING

Most people, when I say that I paint on silk, say, 'Oh, silk-screen printing ...' As you have by now discovered, painting on silk is a one-off process whereby a single image is painted onto the silk itself. Screen-printing, on the other hand, is a means of making a stencil on a screen sometimes made from silk, and then pushing colour through it to make multiple copies of the same image. These repeated images can be made onto paper or any fabric, including silk.

This chapter shows you how silk paints can be thickened enough to print with, and yet still keep their translucent and penetrating qualities.

Printing is a much more sophisticated process than can be detailed here. Therefore this is not an exhaustive explanation of printing techniques. As this book is primarily concerned with silk painting, this chapter shows you ways in which various methods of printing can be combined with painting. It covers some of the most basic ways of printing and stencilling, using materials you can easily

obtain or already have on hand at home.

The variations outlined here relate to how a screen, stamp or stencil can be made, the types of paint which can be used with them, and the ways of doing the printing.

Printing includes the use of other types of stencil besides a silk-screen. In stencilling, paint is pushed or sprayed through gaps, or around solid spaces, onto the surface to be printed. The other main kind of printing discussed in this chapter is stamping, which can be done with an object specifically made for the purpose or with ordinary household items. In this method the stamp object is pressed into the paint, or paint is rolled onto it, and then it is pressed onto the surface to transfer colour to the fabric.

I have found it great fun to share my knowledge of painting with Pauline Clack's expertise in screen-printing to produce fabrics such as the two illustrated on page 16. Overprinting painted fabric is one of the simplest ways to enhance the beauty of your silk by adding greater detail and precision.

Materials for basic screen-printing

◆ blender, if using carragem as a thickening agent

◆ blanket, and/or sheets or some other smooth cushioning surface

◆ carragem, 4 tablespoons, available from craft suppliers, or the commercial thickening agent sold with the paints (the amount of thickener needed depends on how many colours you wish to thicken and use)

◆ Campden tablets, available from craft suppliers) or antiseptic for preserving the carragem solution, if you wish to store it

◆ container, 1 L (2 pt), in which to mix up the carragem

◆ designs, as described in 'Chapter 2', but note comments below

◆ gloves, thin disposable type, or barrier cream

◆ litho paper, or silk-screen stencil paper (shiny and water-resistant on at least one side), at least one sheet

◆ masking tape

◆ old newspapers

◆ paints or dyes diluted and tested as in 'Chapter 4'

Note: these colours will be mixed with a thickening agent which can dilute them further. Therefore they can be mixed with the thickener undiluted, and even in powder form.

◆ pencil

◆ rags or sponges

◆ silk: a piece to be printed, and scraps for testing

◆ silk-screen, bought ready-made from craft suppliers

◆ squeegee, bought ready-made from craft suppliers

◆ Stanley knife

◆ tablespoon

◆ teaspoons, one for each colour

◆ water

Materials for Variations

◆ antifusant

◆ fabric printing inks (see 'Brand Names')

◆ gutta pens filled with water-based gutta in various colours

◆ sprayer (old laundry type, or even an airbrush if available)

◆ cardboard cutouts

◆ masking tape

◆ photographic emulsion and light source (*or* seek professional help)

◆ Riso paper, available from craft suppliers, and heat transfer machine (see 'Brand Names')

◆ screening lacquer and remover

◆ stencils made from objects such as plastic or wire mesh, lace, leaves, plates, uncooked rice, uncooked spaghetti (for use with spraying not printing)

◆ any household items such as sponges, brushes, string, plastic or wire mesh, even scrunched-up plastic food wrap can be used as a stamp

◆ commercial rubber stamps, linocuts, wood blocks, potato cuts or even carved balsa wood made specifically for this purpose

◆ old stamp pads, fine flat sponges, a glass sheet or old plastic or laminated chopping board

THICKENING THE SILK PAINTS

The commercial thickener which comes with some brands of silk paint is simple to use: just follow the directions on the bottle. However, it is much more expensive than mixing your own thickener using carragem, so use the following recipe if you are planning on doing a lot of printing.

◆1. Place 1 - 2 tablespoons of carragem powder in a blender. The amount depends on the amount of thickened paint you need for your printing project.

Note: It is possible to mix up a large batch of carragem and keep it in a sealed jar until you wish to use it. In this case it is useful to mix in a preservative – see step 6 below.

◆ 2. Add 1 - 2 tablespoons of cold water and

mix it with the carragem to form a paste.

✦ 3. Switch the blender on and slowly add more water until the paste starts to become transparent.

✦ 4. Slowly add lukewarm water, blending all the time, until the mixture is semi-liquid, and mostly transparent. Do not add too much water: the mixture needs to remain about the consistency of toothpaste. It can be a little thinner if you are going to be adding dry powder dye rather than pre-mixed paint.

✦ 5. Blend for another minute or two.

✦ 6. Add the dissolved Campden tablet or a teaspoon of antiseptic if you will be storing the carragem solution for any length of time.

✦ 7. In separate jars, add the paint to spoonfuls of the carragem mix until you have the colours you want in the quantities you need. You can use undiluted paint straight from the bottle, or colours diluted and mixed according to the steps in 'Chapter 4', noting that the carragem solution will dilute them a little more. If you are using powder dyes, mix the powder straight into the carragem.

✦ 8. Ensure that the finished product is about the consistency of hair gel. Do not make it too liquid, as the paint will run out through the holes in the screen and bleed into fuzzy lines.

DESIGNING FOR SCREEN-PRINTING

The type of cutout stencil described here is based on the principle that wherever you have cut a hole, the paint will be pushed through onto the fabric. Therefore, your design must be based on blocks or lines of paint which can first be made by cutting out blocks and lines on the litho paper to form a stencil.

✦ You need to make your total design smaller than the silk-screen, of a size that allows a border of at least 2 cm (1 in) all around. This is important because you must have a space where you can dump the paint at the end of each pull across the screen.

✦ If you have not tried screen-printing before it is a good idea to use a design which only uses one colour for your first try, because of the difficulty of 'registering' each colour so that it fits into the right place in the design. Single-colour printing can then be combined with painting the fabric, either before or after printing, to give it more life. The fabrics illustrated on page 16 were first painted by the mop-up method explained in 'Chapter 9', and then printed over the top with fabric paint.

✦ In the method using a cutout stencil described here, it is important that your design be simple enough to ensure that you do not have cutouts within cutouts, in which case your stencil will fall apart. It is possible to stick little bits back onto the screen when you have coated it with paint, but it is best not to start this way if you can help it.

SCREEN-PRINTING TECHNIQUE

✦ 1. Draw your design in pencil onto the litho paper, shiny side up.

✦ 2. Cut the design out carefully with the Stanley knife.

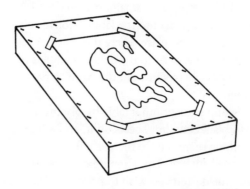

Attaching the stencil to the screen

✦ 3. Attach the litho paper cutout to the outside bottom of the silk-screen, with the shiny side facing the bottom of the screen. Use a tiny piece of masking tape to attach it at each corner, making sure it is as flush with the screen as possible: any potential folds and creases must be smoothed out or paint will leak around the edges.

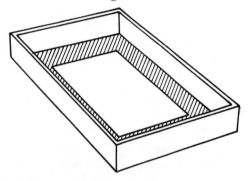

Apply masking tape around the inside edges

✦ 4. Turn the screen over, and stick masking tape around the edges of the bottom of the screen on the inside, so that there is no gap between the litho paper and the sides of the screen. This tape guards against paint being printed through the screen around the edges of the litho paper. It also acts as a reservoir onto which you can dump excess paint after each pull.

✦ 5. Ensure there are no places around the edges of the litho paper where there is a gap in the masking tape, where paint can pass through the screen onto the fabric. Conversely, ensure there is no place where the masking tape covers up the deliberate holes of the stencil, where you want the paint to pass through.

✦ 6. Set up your printing table by placing a folded blanket and/or sheets on it, and smoothing them out, so there is a flat cushioned surface. This should be at least the size of the design you wish to print, or ideally the size of the total piece of fabric if you want to do repeating patterns.

✦ 7. Cover the blanket and/or sheets with several layers of newspaper, again arranged so that there are no folds and creases. Any lump in the cushioning material will cause a line or pale spot in your printing.

✦ 8. Place your screen flat upon the topmost sheet of newspaper, with the litho paper touching the newspaper.

✦ 9. Place several teaspoons of thickened paint onto the screen, on top of the area protected by masking tape, at the top of the screen (the end furthest away from you).

✦ 10. Hold the screen firmly with one hand, so that it does not move. Press down hard so that it cannot shift. *Note:* Screen-printing is much easier if you have a friend to help you do this, but it is possible to do alone, as long as you do not have too big a screen.

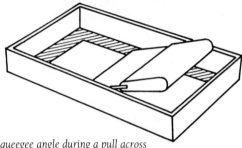

Squeegee angle during a pull across

✦ 11. Take the squeegee in your other hand and hold it on the screen at or above where you placed the paint. Hold it so that it is at an angle to the screen, as illustrated.

✦ 12. Push down hard with the squeegee, still keeping it at an angle to the screen, and pull it across the screen through the paint, so that you drag the paint across the screen, and it prints out onto the newspaper.

✦ 13. Wipe the excess paint off the squeegee by scraping it on the edge of the screen. Pick it up again on the edge of the squeegee.

✦ 14. Pull the paint across the screen again and again, pressing down hard each time, until you can see the stencil clearly through the paint after you have finished a pull.

✦ 15. Carefully lift the screen off the newspaper so that the printed paint underneath does not blur.

✦ 16. Check the practice print on the newspaper to see if there are any places where paint is leaking through. If there are spots of paint which should not be there at all, repair your stencil with more litho paper, or with masking tape, to cover the holes. If there are streaks and blobs running out from the edges of the stencil, this is probably because of folds and creases in the stencil itself. In this case, unstick the edges of the stencil and smooth down any creases and bubbles. By this time the paint should be gluing the stencil to the screen so that you can run your finger over any lumpy bits and smooth them out, from the centre to the edge of the stencil.

✦ 17. If the colour has printed unevenly, put more paint onto the screen, and practice pulling it across the screen with a very strong downward push as you go. Check each time that you have spread the paint all over the screen so that some has gone through all the holes in your stencil. This means pulling the paint across several times, in each direction, before you consider the print finished, and take the screen off.

✦ 18. Throw away the piece of newspaper that has wet paint on it.

Note: Any wet paint which gets onto the bottom of the screen will 'print' onto the silk if you do not wipe it off first, so check the bottom of the screen after each print, and before you put it down on the silk.

✦ 19. Do as many practice prints on clean pieces of newspaper as are necessary to get a good print.

✦ 20. Remove all sheets of newspaper that have been contaminated by paint, and leave a smooth cushioned surface of blankets and/or sheets covered by several layers of clean newspaper.

✦ 21. Place the silk on this surface and smooth it flat. Stick it down tightly with tape just catching the corners.

✦ 22. Carefully position the screen on the silk and print the colour by repeating steps 8 - 15.

✦ 23. If you have a repeating design, repeat this process until the silk is printed all over.

Note: Cover the freshly printed areas of the silk with clean paper where necessary to ensure the paint does not contaminate the base of the screen, or get blurred or smeared by the screen.

✦ 24. Peel the printed silk carefully away from the newspaper-covered cushioning, and place it flat, or pegged on the line at all four corners, to dry. Do this in such a way as to ensure that paint from one part of it does not touch another and smear or transfer.

✦ 25. As soon as you have finished printing, remove the stencil carefully from the screen. Hose the screen down thoroughly to remove any particles of paint, as these can clog the screen if left to dry. If you want to re-use the stencil, allow it to dry flat: make sure it is completely dry before storing it carefully between two sheets of paper or plastic. Weight it down to keep it flat.

✦ 26. Allow the drying silk to dry completely.

✦ 27. Let the silk rest, and then fix the colour by any of the methods in 'Chapter 5'.

✦ 28. In the normal washing and rinsing process after fixing you may need to scrub the silk a little more or use washing soda to remove all the stiffness of the thickener.

VARIATIONS OF THE SCREEN AND STENCIL

Screens can be made in several other ways, including:

✦ Making a photographic image into an emulsion painted directly onto the screen. This requires a good light source to expose the image. Screens like this can be made for you by a professional screen-printing firm, or you can try making your own.

✦ Using Riso paper and a heat transfer machine: Riso paper is a plastic mesh which forms a screen when passed through a thermal copier together with a photocopied drawing or design. See 'Brand Names' and the 'List of Suppliers' for details of these kits.

✦ Painting the screen directly with screening lacquer: a special remover is needed to clean the screen afterwards. Both these chemicals are very toxic and should be used with extreme caution: use a suitable respirator.

Stencils can be used without a screen, spraying or painting unthickened paint around them:

✦ Simple stencils can be made by cutting out designs in cardboard, plastic sheeting of various thicknesses, or 'frisk film'. Frisk film is a slightly tacky plastic film used in air-brushing: its advantage is that its slight stickiness on one side helps the stencil to adhere closely to the fabric, so that paint does not run under the stencil so easily.

✦ Other objects in the list of 'Materials for Variations' above can be used as stencils as long as you coat the silk with antifusant first, and spray the paint over the objects as outlined in 'Chapter 7'.

VARIATIONS OF THE PAINT

✦ Using any of the techniques described in this book, paint the silk with unthickened silk paints, either before or after screen-printing. *Note:* If you paint after printing, the water in the paint may blur the edges of the printed areas, if you have used thickened silk paints and have not fixed them before overpainting. This will not occur if you use screen-printing inks to do the printing.

✦ Place spoonfuls of *different* colours on the screen (as per step 9 above), and mix them together as you pull them across the screen.

✦ Design a set of stencils that fit together so that you can print two or more colours. You will need to plan this carefully, and set your screen and fabric up so that you can place the screen in exactly the same place each time you print a new colour. This is called 'registering'.

✦ Use fabric printing inks to print with instead of thickened silk paint. These can be used straight from the bottle, as they are designed to be thick enough for printing. One of their disadvantages is opacity and stiffness, which cannot be changed. The other is that they sit on the surface and do not go through to the other side of the silk with any consistency: some brands have a penetrating agent which can be mixed with the paint to solve this problem.

✦ Try printing water-based gutta through a silk-screen. It is quite difficult to get a printed gutta line which is even enough to hold the paint in if you want to use it for the serti method (see 'Introduction'). You may have to pull the squeegee across the screen many more times, and press down more firmly, than you would for normal printing. It helps to have a flexible screen such as those available with the Riso paper kits, so that you can bend one corner up to see if the gutta has penetrated right through to the cushioning material, while still maintaining the registration. Even then, it is wise to go over some parts of the line with a gutta pen. Alternatively, you can use the printed gutta purely as a decoration before or after painting. The metallic serti guttas are particularly pretty used this way.

✦ Paint the silk with antifusant before printing to ensure a finer, harder line at the edge of the printed colour.

✦ Use antifusant to cover the silk before spraying unthickened paint through a stencil on a screen or over a stencil. The antifusant will help to ensure that the outline of the stencil is preserved, although the paint will bleed a little if it is unthickened.

✦ Paint unthickened paint through a stencil on the screen, using a paintbrush. Hold the screen down tightly as you do this. Try it with and without a coating of antifusant on the silk. You will not get a clear 'print' this way, but some hints of shape will emerge.

✦ Use a stippling brush or other hard-bristled brush to stipple thickened paint onto the silk through a screen or other stencil.

✦ Use a toothbrush to splatter unthickened paint around a stencil. The effect is better if the silk has been coated with antifusant first.

BASIC STAMPING

Almost any object to which paint will adhere can be used as a stamp. Try household items such as those in the list of 'Materials for Variations'. The paint will need to be thickened as for screen-printing if you want a sharp image to be made from the stamp.

✦ 1. Place your silk on a cushioned surface, as for screen-printing, steps 6, 7 and 21 above.

✦ 2. Mix up thickened paints, as for screen-printing.

✦ 3. Spread colour thinly onto an old stamp pad, a fine flat sponge (without large holes), a sheet of glass or old plastic, or a laminated chopping board.

✦ 4. Press your stamp into the paint, rocking it a little to ensure an even coating.

✦ 5. Place the stamp on the silk and press gently onto the fabric. Place an even pressure all over the stamp and, if necessary, rock it a little to ensure all the surfaces of the stamp transfer paint to the silk. Be careful doing this because you may end up printing from the edges of the stamp, which are not parts of your design.

✦ 6. Pick up the stamp, and repeat steps 4 and 5 until you have stamped your design wherever you want it on the silk.

✦ 7. Allow the paint to dry completely.

✦ 8. Let the silk rest, and then fix and wash according to the instructions in 'Chapter 5'.

Variations

✦ Paint the silk with unthickened paint either before or after stamping.

Note: If you paint after stamping, the water in the paint may blur the edges of the printed areas, if you have used thickened silk paints and have not fixed them before overpainting.

✦ Use fabric printing inks instead of thickened silk paints.

✦ Soak objects such as wool, string, pieces of blotting paper, or any other material that absorbs silk paint, either thickened or not. (You will get an entirely different effect in each case.) Place these objects onto the silk and let them dry there. The paint in them will leave marks on the silk. A different effect is achieved if you place them on white silk, silk which has been painted and dried, or silk which has been painted and is still wet.

✦ Do the above, but instead of leaving the objects to dry in one place, move them around on the silk slowly, leaving trails of paint.

✦ Instead of soaking the *objects* in paint, place them on silk which is still wet from painting, and leave them there while the paint dries; they will soak up paint. The result will be paler places in the silk where the objects were.

✦ You can also cover the silk with a coat of antifusant, and let it dry, before trying any of the above variations. The effects in each case will be different from those on silk not so treated.

✦

13

AUSTRALIAN DESIGNS

This chapter contains some specific designs taken from the Australian environment. Each has been shown as a completed scarf in the colour plates. Line drawings for you to enlarge and copy onto the silk are given in this section, together with step-by-step instructions for painting.

I am not very good at copying, so I find it easier to take each of the line drawings and enlarge it on a photocopier, then trace it onto the silk in pencil or gutta. The drawings are deliberately made as simple as possible, so that they can be used by beginners, and to ensure that all the gutta lines join to enclose the spaces and keep the colour in. You will see in the photographs of the finished items that I have added embellishments and sketchy lines to make them look more sophisticated. You can do this too, but get the simple lines down first so that you avoid bleeds.

It is a good idea first to re-read the appropriate parts of 'Chapter 3' to refresh your memory about using gutta, particularly when tracing designs. Similarly, skim the parts of 'Chapter 4' about basic painting techniques. Remember to test out your colours on scraps of silk, or on a test piece, before applying them to your project silk.

Materials
✦ cotton buds
✦ designs shown in this chapter, enlarged on a photocopier if possible
✦ eye-dropper
✦ thin disposable gloves or barrier cream
✦ gutta pens filled according to instructions in 'Chapter 3', with size 6 or 7 nibs: one with black spirit-based gutta and one with clear spirit-based gutta
✦ hair dryer (optional)
✦ paints or dyes, diluted and tested according to 'Chapter 4'
✦ paintbrushes, a selection of sizes
✦ rags, tissues or paper towels
✦ silk on a frame, prepared according to 'Chapter 2'
✦ silk scraps, or test piece on a small frame
✦ water

Materials for Variations
✦ fine black marking pen
✦ masking tape
✦ paper: sheets as large as the designs you wish to achieve
✦ pencil and eraser
✦ slides
✦ slide projector

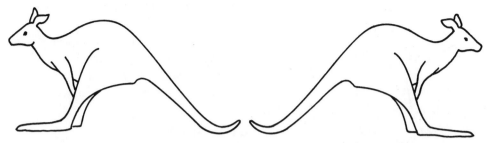

'Kangaroos' design

'KANGAROOS'

See colour plate on page 10.

✦ 1. Draw a border according to the instructions in 'Chapter 3'.

✦ 2. Copy or trace a kangaroo onto each corner of the silk with black gutta, according to the instructions in 'Chapter 3'.

✦ 3. Decorate inside the kangaroos with a very fine patterning of black gutta. I have used designs reminiscent of Aboriginal bark paintings.

✦ 4. Between the kangaroos draw gutta circles, using lines and dots of gutta, some in black and some in clear.

✦ 5. Check that all gutta lines are thick enough to retain the paint, and that there are no gaps in the lines or at the joins.

✦ 6. Let the gutta dry for a minute or two.

✦ 7. Using a very fine brush, paint the colours inside the gutta designs in the kangaroos and circles. Rest your arm on the side of the frame to steady it when you are filling in very small spaces, and do not have very much paint on the brush. I have used earth colours in my scarf.

✦ 8. Paint the background using a large brush with a fine tip, or with a foambrush, filling in the corners around the gutta designs with a smaller brush. Re-read the section in 'Chapter 4' on backgrounds first, if you need to.

✦ 9. Paint the border, using a large brush or a foambrush. Paint quickly for a smooth finish.

✦ 10. Allow the paint to dry completely before removing the silk from the frame.

✦ 11. Let the silk rest, and then fix and wash according to the instructions in 'Chapter 5'.

'LORIKEETS'

See colour plate on page 11.

✦ 1. Use a long scarf for this design so that you can put lorikeets at each end.

✦ 2. Draw a border with gutta according to the instructions in 'Chapter 3'.

✦ 3. Copy or trace the lorikeets onto each end of the silk with gutta according to the instructions in 'Chapter 3'.

✦ 4. Decorate the lines a little by adding sketchy lines and shadings with gutta to the simple outlines.

✦ 5. Check that all gutta lines are thick enough to retain the paint, and that there are no gaps in the lines or at the joins.

✦ 6. Let the gutta dry for a minute or two.

✦ 7. Using a fine brush, paint dark blue on the beak ridge and eye.

✦ 8. Wash the brush in water and then paint red onto the beak and the eyeline. Shade a reddish pink into the red of the eyeline while it is still wet.

✦ 9. Use a medium brush to paint a mid-blue onto the head.

✦ 10. While the blue is still wet, blend bright green into it at the edge of the wings. Continue the green down the wings.

✦ 11. While the blue on the head is still damp, take a very fine brush and paint some lines of green into the blue.

✦ 12. While the green of the wings is still

'Lorikeets' design

damp, take a fine brush with very little paint on it and paint dark green and blue shadings onto the wings.

✦ 13. Use a medium brush to paint a blob of red onto the chest.

✦ 14. Quickly wash the brush and use it to shade yellow around the top of the red while it is still wet.

✦ 15. Wash the brush again and use it to shade purple into the bottom of the red while it is still damp.

✦ 16. Use the same technique to shade blue into the purple of the tail.

✦ 17. Add embellishments of lines and shadings of complementary colours over the colours already laid down. Use a fine brush with very little paint on it to do this. Some paint can be added when the base colour is damp, for merging colours, and some can be added when the base colour is dry, for hard lines of texture.

✦ 18. Paint the background as in step 8 for 'Kangaroos'.

✦ 19. Paint the border, using a large brush or a

foambrush. Paint quickly to ensure a smooth finish.

✦ 20. Allow the paint to dry completely before removing the silk from the frame.

✦ 21. Let the silk rest, and then fix and wash according to instructions in 'Chapter 5'.

'GUM BLOSSOM'

This is the same design used in 'Chapter 7'. You will find it very different to paint it onto silk without the antifusant, using gutta instead. See colour plates on pages 10 and 13.

✦ 1. Draw a border with gutta according to the instructions in 'Chapter 3'.

✦ 2. Copy or trace the gum blossom design onto a square of silk with gutta, according to the instructions in 'Chapter 3'.

✦ 3. Decorate the lines a little by adding sketchy lines and shadings with gutta to the simple outlines.

✦ 4. Check that all gutta lines are thick enough to retain the paint, and that there are no gaps in the lines or at the joins. This is particularly important on the blossoms themselves, so draw lots of sketchy lines as the stamens, and then join up any gaps by making exaggerated circles for the pollen grains.

✦ 5. Let the gutta dry for a minute or two.

✦ 6. Using a fine brush, paint fine lines of pink onto all the gum blossom, following the gutta lines you have drawn as stamens. Be careful to stay inside the outermost gutta lines.

✦ 7. If you find that there are gaps in the gutta you have missed and the paint is bleeding through, quickly add more pollen circles to the design to contain the bleeds.

✦ 8. Wash the brush in water and then paint fine lines of purple next to and over the pink. Do some of these while the pink is still damp, and some where it is dry, to get texture. You can dry the paint with a hair dryer to speed this process.

✦ 9. Use a clean fine brush to paint yellow into the pollen dots. If there are bleeds, quickly add

'Gum Blossom' design

more gutta dots, as in step 7. You may need to dry the paint first and seal any gaps in existing gutta lines, if you are getting too many pollen dots.

◆ 10. Use light brown on a fine brush to paint the first coat on the stems, leaf veins and nuts. Leave these to dry.

◆ 11. Paint the central point in each flower with yellow.

◆ 12. While the light brown is drying, take a medium brush with very little paint on it and paint green-gold inside all the leaf shapes.

◆ 13. Quickly wash the brush and use it to

shade dark green into the leaves. Do not have much paint on the brush or it will overtake the green-gold.

◆ 14. Wash the brush again and shade in yellow, golden brown and darker brown while the green-gold is still drying, so that some of the colours blend, and others make sharper lines as the base colour dries out more.

◆ 15. Use the same technique to shade darker colours into the stems and nuts.

◆ 16. Paint the border first this time because it is a lighter colour than the background. Use a large brush or a foambrush. Paint quickly to ensure a smooth finish.

✦ 17. Paint the background as you did in step 8 for 'Kangaroos'.

✦ 18. Allow the paint to dry completely before removing the silk from the frame.

✦ 19. Let the silk rest, and then fix and wash according to the instructions in 'Chapter 5'.

'COCKATOOS'

See colour plate on page 12.

✦ 1. Copy or trace each cockatoo with gutta onto the four corners of a square of silk,

according to the instructions in 'Chapter 3'. Do this before you do the border so that you can make some of the wing tips and tailfeathers go over the border: this adds an element of interest to the design. Be careful not to take these parts so close to the edge of the silk that they will have to be cut off when you are sewing the scarf: they need to be well inside the staple or pin lines of the frame.

✦ 2. Draw a border with gutta, according to the instructions in 'Chapter 3'.

✦ 3. Decorate the lines a little with the gutta,

'Cockatoos' design

by adding sketchy lines and shadings to the simple outlines.

✦ 4. Check that all gutta lines are thick enough to retain the paint, and that there are no gaps in the lines or at the joins. This is particularly important on the cockatoos themselves, because they are mostly white and any bleeds from the background will be very noticeable.

✦ 5. Let the gutta dry for a minute or two.

✦ 6. Using a medium brush, paint clean water inside all of the cockatoos, except on the crests. Be careful to stay inside the outermost gutta lines. Use this as a way to check whether there are going to be any bleeds: if water seeps out, paint will too. If water does seep out, dry the silk and repair the gutta line. Then repaint the cockatoos with water, as this is needed to blend in the yellows.

✦ 7. Paint yellow in the crests, and in fine lines over the damp silk at the points where there are shadings on the feathers. Use more water to blend these in where appropriate. Both the yellow paint for the shadows and the extra water for blending should be applied sparingly, with very little water or paint on the brush.

✦ 8. When the cockatoos have dried, paint the beaks and feet with a fine brush dipped in grey.

✦ 9. Paint the branches and leaves following steps 10 - 15 for the 'Gum Blossom' scarf.

✦ 10. Paint the background following step 8 for 'Kangaroos'. Paint small enclosed areas first, and then paint the large areas with a big brush.

✦ 11. Let the background dry, and then apply clean water all over it with an eye-dropper. Remember to touch the silk with the eye-dropper and to place lots of drops closely together.

✦ 12. Paint the border using a large brush or a foambrush. Paint quickly to ensure a smooth finish.

✦ 13. Allow the paint to dry completely before removing the silk from the frame.

✦ 14. Let the silk rest, and then fix and wash according to the instructions in 'Chapter 5'.

VARIATIONS

You may want to develop your own designs. A very simple way to do this is to take colour slides of plants, animals or places, and trace a projection of the image (see 'Designing Your Painting', page 25). This is the way I did the 'Gum Blossom' design.

✦

14

FINISHING OFF AND ITEMS TO MAKE

Once you have painted the silk with the dyes or paints there are still many things you can do to decorate your work and, of course, you need to make it into something, even if it is just a matter of sewing around the edges to create a scarf, or attaching it to a hanging device so that you can put it on the wall.

DECORATION

One of the simplest ways to turn a dull painting into an interesting one is to embellish the design with fabric pens, and with coloured and metallic guttas. Guttas can be used to decorate before or after painting, but the fabric pens need to be done last or the wet paint may smear them. Of course, a smeary blurred design may be just what you are looking for.

Materials

+ cotton buds, rags, tissues or paper towelling
+ fabric pens, several colours, or at least black
+ gloves, thin disposable ones, or barrier cream
+ 2 gutta pens filled with gutta according to directions in 'Chapter 3': one with black spirit-based gutta, one with gold water-based gutta

+ eye-droppers, preferably 2, but 1 is sufficient
+ silk paints or dyes, diluted and tested according to instructions in 'Chapter 4'
+ silk on a frame, prepared according to instructions in 'Chapter 2'
+ water

Materials for Variations

+ adhesive fabric paints in applicator bottles
+ embroidery and sewing threads and needles, or sewing machine
+ beads, sequins, decorative buttons and studs
+ fabric paints, several colours, or at least metallic gold
+ feathers, bones, sticks, shells and other objects
+ fringing
+ fusible webbing
+ masking tape
+ overlocker (optional)
+ paintbrushes, a selection of sizes
+ pegs
+ pins
+ sheets of plastic, or a laminated workbench or table

DECORATING WITH FABRIC PENS AND GUTTA

The scarf illustrated on page 8 was painted in earth tones, with flowers drawn over the paint in black fabric pen. You can use the same method to make a scarf in any colour scheme, and with designs other than flowers.

✦ 1. Paint the silk using the wet on wet technique with an eye-dropper, described in 'Chapter 6'.

✦ 2. As they dry, the drops of colour will blend and form shapes which will suggest design ideas to you. I found flowers were the easiest to do. I used a fine black fabric pen, once the paint was dry, to quickly sketch flower petals onto the painted silk; basically outlining areas of different colour, but not following them exactly if it meant that the shape no longer looked like a flower.

✦ 3. Sketch rapidly so that the pen does not rest in one place too long and make a blob of colour, but also press down firmly so that a distinct line is drawn.

✦ 4. Let the silk rest, and then fix and wash according to the instructions in 'Chapter 5'. *Note*: Many fabric pens and fabric paints are not dry-cleanable and therefore cannot be washed in white spirit. You will need to test this on a scrap of silk if you want to use them in conjunction with clear spirit-based gutta. The other alternative is to draw your clear spirit-based gutta lines so finely that you do not need to rinse the gutta out.

Variations

✦ Use opaque fabric paints, silk paints or dyes thickened with carragem, and silk-screening inks to decorate. Apply these with paintbrushes, stamps or through a screen-printing method as described in 'Chapter 12'. You can also fill a gutta pen with these paints, and draw them on as you would gutta, but you will need to use a large nib, preferably size 8, and dilute them with water first.

✦ Colour clear water-based gutta with the silk paints or dyes, and apply this with a gutta pen.

✦ Paint onto a jacquard silk with a simple wash of colour or with the mop-up technique from 'Chapter 9', and then outline the pattern woven into the silk, using coloured gutta, fabric pens or thicker paints.

ADDING TRIMMINGS

A great variety of trimmings can be added to your creations. Your imagination is the only limit here.

✦ Attach beads, sequins, decorative buttons or studs, feathers, bones, shells, sticks or any other objects which might appeal to you. These are best sewn on, but many can be glued with a tacky craft glue, especially if the item is not going to be washed. Iron-on sequins, available from some craft and sewing shops, are an easy way to go, but you need to be careful that you get them in the right place the first time, as they are absolutely fixed once ironed down!

✦ Attach fringing to the edges of the silk. Another alternative is to fringe the edge of the silk itself by using a needle to work threads loose, and then pull them out. If you want to do this on the selvedge side of the silk, cut or rip the selvedge off first.

✦ Embroider and/or quilt the silk, either in small areas to emphasise parts of the design, or all over, using traditional methods. Do this by hand or by machine.

✦ Appliqué small pieces of painted silk to larger pieces, or to other fabrics, including ready-made clothes. This can be done using traditional methods, or by the following short cuts.

✦ If the piece to be appliquéd is a simple shape, use an overlocker with a rolled hem plate to sew round the edges with a very small stitch length and width. Attach this to the base fabric using an iron-on fusible webbing. Then sew down the edges using a small zigzag stitch on an ordinary sewing machine: this looks like satin stitch when combined with the overlocked edge.

✦ For more complex shapes you can first attach the silk to the base piece using iron-on fusible webbing. Then to seal the edges to prevent them from fraying and to stick them down, use an adhesive fabric paint, sold in an applicator pen at craft suppliers. Simply draw a line around all the edges, half on the silk, and half on the base fabric, and let this dry over several hours.

Note: It is not easy to achieve a fine line with these adhesive fabric pens at first, so practise a little. If you are attaching fine silk to fine silk or other thin fabric, the paint will go right through both layers and will smear easily if you move it while the paint is still wet, so tape or pin the silk down tightly. Do not have a layer of paper under the fabrics, because the fabric paint will adhere strongly to the paper: use sheets of plastic, or a laminated tabletop instead.

PERMANENT PLEATS OR CREASING

The silk can be permanently pleated or creased to add dimension or texture. Fabric treated in this way will maintain the pleats and creases through washing, but will keep them more successfully if you refold or retwist them and hang them on the line to dry this way, after each washing. It is best to paint and fix the colour in the silk first, because the steaming which sets the pleats or creases does not always do a good job of setting the colour, because of the bulkiness of the silk.

✦ 1. Fold the silk into pleats and sew these into place at the ends, or twist it into a tight sausage shape and tie or sew the ends.

✦ 2. Roll this in paper and steam it for 2 hours, according to the instructions in 'Chapter 5'. You will only be able to steam a few pieces at a time this way.

✦ 3. Leave the fabric still sewn or tied in place for at least 24 hours after the steaming, to settle in the creases.

FINISHING OFF

Anything you can make out of fabric can be made out of painted silk. All you need to do is to choose the weight of silk best suited to the object you have in mind. Here are some ideas, some of which you can see illustrated in the photographs in this book.

SCARVES, SHAWLS, RIBBONS, PLACEMATS AND TABLECLOTHS

All sorts of things can be made from simple squares and rectangles. These are finished off by simply hemming around the edges, either by hand or on a sewing machine. I use an overlocker which has a rolled hem plate, using a very small stitch, and stretch the silk tight with both hands, in both directions at once, so that it goes through the machine without puckering. See colour plate on page 14.

White silk scarves can be bought already hand-rolled. The only drawback to these is that you must sew them to the frame or use very fine pins. Anything rougher, like staples, will leave permanent holes in the silk.

Shawls look very nice with a fringe added by buying commercially produced fringing, and sewing it on, or by fringing the silk itself. This latter method can be used with all sizes of scarves, but the sewn-on fringing looks better with the largest sizes, as it is quite bulky.

Placemats and tablecloths are best done in heavier weight silks. Lighter silks need to be glued to cardboard or wooden backings for place mats, but be careful that the glue is applied sparingly so that it does not show through the fine fabric. Alternatively you can try laminating the silk for these purposes. Many laminating companies are not willing to try to do this because it is almost impossible to do without creasing the silk and having those creases immortalised in the plastic. For place mats, this is solved by first gluing the silk to a firm backing, such as cardboard.

WALLHANGINGS

Silk paintings can be really lovely hung on the wall, or in a window where the sun will shine through them like stained glass. Unfortunately, the life of a painting hung in the window is shortened because direct sunlight will eventually fade the colours.

You can strengthen your silk before making it into a wallhanging by sewing it together with some other stronger fabric such as cotton, as a backing material. This will mean the light will not shine through it very well, if you are thinking of hanging it in the window.

The quickest way to turn your painting into a wallhanging is to buy two pieces of poster-hanger plastic and insert the silk as you would a poster. If you are not sewing it onto backing material first, it is a good idea to hem the silk all the way around, as you would a scarf, to prevent fraying.

Another way is to hem the silk closely on the two sides, and then make 1 - 2 cm ($\frac{1}{2}$ - 1 in) hems on the top and bottom. Leave the sides of these two hems open, so that you can insert pieces of rounded dowelling, or plastic rods, into the top and the bottom. Tie some picture wire or pretty cord to the ends of the top rod, to hang the picture.

Your silk can be framed to hang on the wall: either buy your own and do it yourself, or take it to a commercial framer.

CUSHION COVERS

See colour plate on page 2.

Cushion covers are lovely things to make out of painted silk, because you can paint a picture and have the whole of it showing on the face of the cushion.

✦ 1. Cut your painted silk into two squares big enough to take the cushion you have in mind, adding a generous seam allowance of about 1.5 cm ($\frac{5}{8}$ in). If you have not painted enough silk for two squares, you can always use another colour-coordinated fabric to act as the

back. To strengthen your cover, it is a good idea to attach these two squares to a stronger fabric as a backing.

✦ 2. Place the two squares of silk, or silk plus backing material, with right sides facing, and pin or tack them together on three sides, along the line of the seam allowances (that is, in a straight line about 1.5 cm ($\frac{5}{8}$ in) from the edge, parallel to each of the three sides).

✦ 3. Check that you can insert the cushion so that it fits properly into the cover, and repin or tack the seams if you have made the cover too big or too small.

✦ 4. Sew the seams together, and then cut off the excess fabric diagonally across the corner seam allowances, making sure not to cut too close to the stitching.

✦ 5. Insert the cushion and turn in the seam allowance on the last side. Carefully sew this side closed, using a slip-stitch that you can barely see.

Variations

The trouble with this last method is that in order to wash the cushion you have to undo your careful sewing to remove the cushion. Therefore it is better to insert a zip into the last side, or velcro strips, although this material can be too stiff for the finer silks.

✦ Add piping around the edges for a neater finish: instructions for this come with commercially available sewing patterns, but it is quite difficult to do with the slippery finer silks.

✦ Insert wadding between the silk and the backing material, and quilt it a little to add emphasis to your design and to attach the three layers together evenly. Then sew your cushion up as above.

LAMPSHADES

Painted silk makes gorgeous lampshades, because the light shines through them with a glow which lights up the design. You will need a straight-sided lampshade frame: this consists of two white plastic-coated circles of the same size, one with an attachment for the globe socket. They are available from craft suppliers. You also need spray adhesive, glue, double-sided adhesive tape approximately 1 cm (¹/₂ in) wide, scissors, a cardboard roll, and lampshade backing material.

The silk needs to be glued to the lampshade backing material. You must apply a very even, fine layer of glue because it has a tendency to go right through the finer silks and show up as wet-looking marks: this is why a spray adhesive is best. If you can find it, self-adhesive lampshade backing material makes the job much simpler. However, this type is not readily available, so the best alternative is a lampshade parchment: ask at your craft supplier or lampshade makers.

The backing material needs to be about 3 cm (1¹/₄ in) smaller than the silk all around, but still long enough to fit precisely around the frame of the shade. Therefore you should paint your silk to suit the size of the lampshade frame plus the overlap (or buy a frame that suits the size of silk you have already painted).

✦ 1. Roll the silk onto the cardboard roll to make it easier to smooth it out onto the backing material.

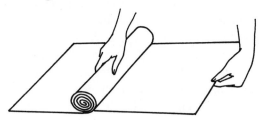

Rolling the silk onto the backing material

✦ 2. Spray one side of the backing material all over with a fine layer of adhesive.

✦ 3. Stretch the silk so that it is wide enough for an equal amount to be overlapping the backing material at the top and bottom. Unroll the silk slowly onto the backing material, as shown, smoothing it down as you go, so that there are no wrinkles or air bubbles.

✦ 4. Stick one side of the double-sided adhesive tape all along the overlapping silk, at the top and bottom of the backing material. Leave the protective backing on the other side of the tape. Trim the outside edge of the silk, so that there is no part where the silk overlaps beyond the outside edge of the tape.

Applying double-sided tape

✦ 5. Spread a thin layer of glue around the outside edge of the plastic-coated frames and along the edge of the backing material on the opposite side to the silk. Be careful not to get any on the covering of the tape.

✦ 6. Place the frame so that the edges are flush with the edge of the lampshade backing material. Roll the silk covered backing material onto the lampshade frame (silk side outwards, of course), glueing it down as you go.

Applying glue to the frame

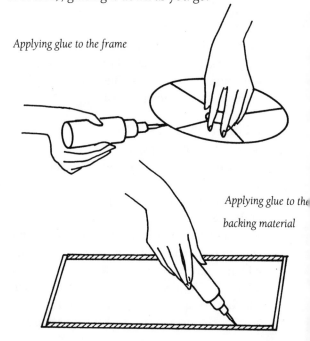

Applying glue to the backing material

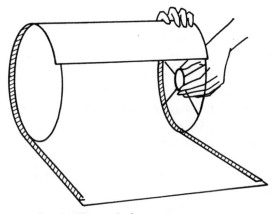

Rolling the silk onto the frame

◆ 7. When you come to the place where the fabric will join with itself to complete the circle of the lampshade, fold the last edge of the silk under so that you will get a smooth 'hem'.

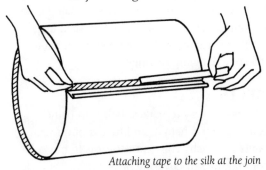

Attaching tape to the silk at the join

◆ 8. Attach double-sided adhesive tape to the already stretched silk, underneath where the join will be. Remove the protective backing from the other side of the tape, and smooth the loose end of the silk down onto it, making sure you catch down the turned-under 'hem'.

◆ 9. Remove the protective backing from the double-sided tape attached to the silk overlap at the top and bottom of the lampshade, and fold it over the frame all around. Push the inside edges up under the inside of the frame using the end of the scissors. The lampshade is finished!

PURSES AND BAGS

See colour plate on page 15.

The heavier-weight silk can make purses and bags without padding: finer silks are best

quilted with wadding before they are sewn up. There are many commercial patterns available, but a very simple one can be made with a drawstring.

◆ 1. Cut two small squares or rectangles of silk, or two semicircular shapes with some extra allowance at the top, as shown.

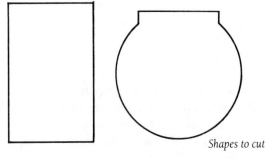

Shapes to cut

◆ 2. Cut two more of the same shapes in a stronger lining material, such as cotton, and in wadding if you are going to quilt the purse.

◆ 3. Join the silk to the lining (with the wadding in between if you are using it) and then place these with the right sides together. Pin or tack the pieces together around the three edges, as you did the cushion cover, leaving 3 cm (1¼ in) open on one side at the top, as illustrated.

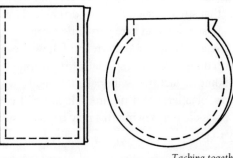

Tacking together

◆ 4. Turn the seam allowances at this opening in to the lining side of the purse and sew them down with fine hand stitches which do not go through to the silk outside of the purse.

◆ 5. Turn the top edge of the purse over onto the lining side a fraction, or overlock it so that it does not fray. Then turn it over again so that there is a 1 cm (¹/₂ in) hem. Sew this down, leaving open the hole to insert a pretty cord to make a drawstring.

BADGES, KEYRINGS AND FRIDGE MAGNETS

See colour plate on page.15.

These can all be made using silk instead of paper as the artwork. You need access to a badge machine: some schools have these for hire or loan, and there are commercial badge-making companies to which you can take your silk: look them up in the phonebook. While not strictly necessary, it is easier if you first stiffen the silk by ironing some interfacing onto the back of it. Be careful: if the iron is too hot the glue will melt right through the silk and make little transparent dots all over your painting.

TIES AND BOW TIES

These are some of the most exciting things to make out of handpainted silk. You need to remember that long ties are cut on the cross, and so your design will need to take into account that the finished product will go diagonally across the silk. Be careful not to use silks that stretch, such as crepe de chine. Bow ties are simpler, and take very little fabric.

Use a commercial pattern and follow the instructions carefully, especially for the long tie. Some tie factories will make up small orders of at least four ties in each fabric: if you are not skilled at sewing this may be the best way to go.

SILK-COVERED BUTTONS AND JEWELLERY

See colour plates on pages 5, 8, 15.

As well as making buttons simply for buttons, I use them as the basis for earrings, brooches, scarf rings, and cufflinks. Self-covering button kits, complete with instructions, can be bought

from the haberdashers. Once you have made up the buttons, cut the shank off the back using wire cutters if the button is metal, or a Stanley knife if the button is made from plastic. If necessary, sand the button back flat with a file, or shave it flat with a Stanley knife if it is plastic. Glue on a suitable back bought from a craft shop. Most craft suppliers have brooch, stud and clip-on earring backs, and ring pads, but cufflink pads are a little harder to find.

Use a glue suitable to the type of button you have made, depending on whether it is plastic or metal. An epoxy resin glue is fine for most, but will occasionally break off at a later time. Use epoxy resin glues with care.

If you are painting silk specifically for button-sized products, remember to suit the size of your design to the size of the finished item.

Plastic tubing stuffed with silk can make effective dangling earrings.

BELTS

The easiest way to make a belt is to paint a long scarf and hem it, and tie it around your waist as a sash. The next easiest is to buy a kit for making self-covering belts, with instructions, from the haberdashers.

Belts of varying complexity can be made by quilting the silk.

✦ 1. Paint and fix the colour into a long piece of silk. Fold it over. Alternatively, use two long pieces and place them together.

✦ 2. Cut a piece of wadding to the size of the folded silk, and sew the silk together around the wadding.

✦ 3. Run some stitching in patterns to quilt the wadding-filled silk.

✦ 4. Add a buckle, or two pieces of silk or cord for tying, and the belt is complete.

OTHER PROJECTS

The uses to which you put your silk are only limited by your imagination. Experiment!

BRAND NAMES

SILK PAINTS

ORIENT EXPRESS

These are the ones I started with, and still use most often. They are made by Pebeo, a French company. Their main advantage for me is the range of 20 pre-mixed colours which I find especially attractive compared to other brands. They are water-based and ready to use from the bottle, although the manufacturers recommend that they be diluted by at least 10 per cent water, or by a mix of 50:50 water:alcohol. They can be fixed by steaming, or by a chemical process, or both. They can be set also by a combination of microwaving and chemical fixative. I find that in each case two processes are better than one to ensure colour fastness.

PEBEO SOIE

Pebeo now also supply this silk paint series, which are really lovely with 80 colours to choose from, and very good colour fastness. These paints are pre-mixed in the bottle and seem to be alcohol- and water-based (a mix of alcohol and water). They can be diluted with water alone, or alcohol and water. The disadvantages are that they are more expensive, are only available in Australia in small bottles, and are recommended to be steamed for 3 hours instead of 2. I have found,

however, that the length of time in steaming can be cut down to 2 hours if the Orient Express chemical fixative is applied after steaming. These paints can also be microwaved and then chemically fixed, but some colour is lost in the process..

OTHER BRANDS

Silk Express, from Batik Oetoro, and Silk Road are two Australian brands which have become available in recent years. Other brands I have tried are Elbesoie, and Princecolour from Marie France. They are all similar to the Orient Express paints, and your choice is more likely to depend on the colours in the pre-mixed range, and whether they are readily available in your area, than on any other differences. I have not tested these for microwaving.

DRIMALAN F

I also paint with these more general dyes which can be used on fabrics other than silk and wool. They are available in powder form, and have to be mixed with water, lyogen and acetic acid (28 drops of each per 1L (2 pt) of water, with 50 g ($1^3/_4$ oz) of the powder). They are extremely colour-fast, intense dyes, and cheaper than the paints. They are steamed for 1 - 2 hours or microwaved and chemically fixed with Orient Express fixative (except that blue and black tend to lose a lot of colour.)

Therefore, they can be used on the same piece of work, or even intermixed with Orient Express paints (provided that the proportions of lyogen and acetic acid are kept within reasonable balance). Their main disadvantages are that the available range of colours is limited, so you have to mix your own secondary and tertiary hues, and that if you do not get the best proportions of dye to water the excess colour can cause difficulties in the fixing process.

DRIMASET

These are pre-mixed liquid dyes from Batik Oetoro. They are for cotton and silk, and can be set by ironing. They are thicker than the silk paints, and therefore do not bleed as easily, although they can be thinned down with special additives to get around this problem. They are paler on silk than on cotton. There are 15 colours available.

To use these successfully on silk, you will also need Drimaset Thinner, Drimaset Dilutant, and DS Liquid in the first wash.

GUTTAS

ORIENT EXPRESS

This brand has clear and black, and metallic silver and gold, in spirit-based gutta. None of these are dry-cleanable, and Pebeo now warn customers not to use the gold or silver on things that are to be washed. Apparently the silver and gold colouring will gradually wash out in water, as well as come out straight away in dry-cleaning fluid. Thus, they say not to use these guttas for anything other than wallhangings, furnishings and so on: things which will rarely, if ever, need to be cleaned. I have found that the gold is worse than the silver in this way, but that the problem is variable: sometimes the gold and silver stay in despite washing, sometimes they do not.

A clear water-based guttta is also available in this brand.

OTHER BRANDS

Each brand has its own series of spirit-based guttas, and I have found the ones I have tried to be much the some as the others, except for the problem with Orient Express metallic guttas mentioned above. Elbesoie metallic spirit-based guttas can be washed. I have not tried the others: check with your supplier.

The only dry-cleanable black gutta I have found is the Shop Text one from France (see 'List of Suppliers').

WATER-BASED GUTTA

Coloured and metallic water-based guttas are dry-cleanable and washable. The Serti ones from Batik Oetoro are especially lovely, but difficult to use (as are all water-based guttas: see 'Chapter 3' for detailed instructions).

Clear water-based guttas are available in most brands. Silk Road have two types which can be diluted with the paints to form coloured gutta: their 'Gutta Kakadu' also has metallic flecks in it which adds another level of beauty to the gutta lines. Their 'Gutta Lagoon' makes an interesting effect when drawn onto silk where the paint is still wet: ghostly paler lines form. These two types are the best brand for diluting with silk paint to make coloured gutta, because they are thicker to begin with.

No doubt other brands of water-based gutta can also be used in this way, and can be mixed with the paints to make coloured lines, but most other water-based guttas are ready to use from the bottle, and need very little dilution with water. Therefore in mixing paint with them it is very easy to over-dilute them.

FABRIC PRINTING INKS AND SCREEN KITS

The most commonly available brands in Australia are Permaset and Harlequin. Both of these are good products, and there is very little practical difference between them.

A newer brand here is Tintex, which has some very interesting additives. The most useful one for printing on silk is the Penetrating Agent, which makes the printed colour go right through the silk, so that it is printed on both sides. This can be very important for scarves, in particular, but be careful: lettering and numbers will be mirror image.

A screen-printing kit, called Print Gocco, is now available in Australia. These kits use Riso paper and a light source to create precise and detailed screens 'in a flash'. An alternative is to use the Riso paper and a thermal copier used in schools and colleges to make overhead projection sheets and printing masters.

MARBLING INKS

Batik Oetoro have a set of fabric marbling inks which work very well.

The Japanese Boku-Undo Marbling Kits are quite difficult to use at first. Although in some ways simpler than mixing up a carragem bath, the use of clear water means that the inks do tend to sink to the bottom. Because the inks have to be extremely fine to stay on the surface at all, a lot of ink needs to be dropped, in quick succession; it cannot be manipulated like the oil-based inks, and in the end a much paler colour is transferred.

Pelikan inks work well on a sizing bath but you can also try them on water in much the same way as the Boku-Undo.

◆

LIST
OF SUPPLIERS

If you don't have a shop near you that can supply
all of the materials you need, look through the
advertisements in the general craft press for up-to-
date names and addresses. Two of the best sources are
Popular Crafts and *Crafts* magazines.

*The UK distributor of Orient
Express and other Pebeo
products is:*
Philip & Tacey
North Way
Andover
Hampshire
SP10 5BA
Tel: (0264) 332171

Riso paper screens:
Riso Europe Ltd
1230 High Road
Whetstone
London
N20 0LH
Tel: (081) 446 1188

◆

SUPPLEMENTARY READING LIST

Books in English

Bruandet, Pierre: Painting *On Silk,* Hobbycraft Books, EP Publishing, Wakefield, West Yorkshire, England, 1982

Dawson, Pam (Ed): *The Art Of Painting On Silk,* Vol 1 and 2, Search Press, Tunbridge Wells, Kent, England, 1987

Rousset, Paulette (Ed): *Silk Painting*, number 1 and 2, translated by Gisela Banbury, Les Editions De Saxe S.A., Lyon Cedex 7, France, 1986

Taylor, Jacqueline: *Painting and Embroidery on Silk,* Cassell, London, 1992

Teasdale, Di (Compiler): *Silk Painting: Techniques And Projects,* Kangaroo Press, Kenthurst, Australia, 1991

Books in French

Bain, Litza: *Guide De La Peinture Sur Soie,* Manu Presse, Dessain Et Tolra, Paris, 1987, 1989

Dorigo, Carmen: *Peindre A Gutta*, Manu Presse, Dessain Et Tolra, Paris, 1984

Libessart, Regine: *Le Livre Complet De La Peinture Sur Soie*, translated from Italian by Sylvie Girard, Editions Fleurus, Paris, 1987

Ottelart, Lydie: *L'Aquarelle Sur Soie*, Manu Presse, Dessain Et Tolra, Paris, 1988, 1989

Ottelart, Lydie: *Nouvelles Techniques Pour La Peinture Sur Soie,* Manu Presse, Dessain Et Tolra, Paris, 1986, 1989

General Craft and Related Matters

De Boer, Janet (Ed): *Dyeing For Fibres And Fabrics,* The Australian Forum For Textile Arts, Ltd, 1987, Kangaroo Press, Kenthurst, Australia, 1989

De Boer, Janet (Ed): *Textile Crafts For Beginners,* The Australian Forum For Textile Arts, Ltd, Kangaroo Press, Kenthurst, Australia, 1989

Deyrup, Astrith: *Getting Started In Batik*, Collier Books, Collier Macmillan Publishers, London, 1974

Grunebaum, Gabrielle: *How To Marbleize Paper,* Dover Publications, Inc, New York, 1984

Kafka, Francis J: Batik, *Tie Dyeing, Stenciling, Silk Screen, Block Printing: The Hand Decoration Of Fabrics,* Dover Publications, Inc, New York, 1959, 1973

Ikuyoshi Shibukawa and Yumi Takahashi: *Designer's Guide To Colour,* Vol 1 2 and 3, Angus And Robertson Publishers, North Ryde, Australia, 1984 (vol 1), 1985 (vol 2), 1986 (vol 3)

Vogel Maurer, Diane, with Maurer, Paul: *Marbling: A Complete Guide To Creating Beautiful Patterned Papers And Fabrics*, A Friedman Group Book, Michael Friedman Publishing Group, Inc, New York 1991

◆

INDEX